LLANBLETHIAN:
BUILDINGS AND PEOPLE

LLANBLETHIAN : BUILDINGS AND PEOPLE

A selection of the buildings of Llanblethian
and the people who have lived in them

COWBRIDGE RECORD SOCIETY
2001

Contributors

Text: Betty Alden, Jeff Alden, Iris Ashby, Margaret Chappell, Sue Collier, Barbara Davies, Barbara Easterbrook, Deborah Fisher, George Haynes, Keith Jones, Marie Makepeace, Keith Morgan, Kay Newham, David Pierce, Richard Press, Mary Provis, Tony Provis, José Rawlins, Gaynor Rees, Rosemary Ryland, Mary Wallis, Christine Young

Photographs: Rhys Thomas, Walter Stone, David James, Pauline Horsey, Alan Hey, Della Deeley, Sue Collier, Cowbridge Museum Trust (pp Joyce Williams), Eurion Brown, John Andrews, Jeff Alden

Editor: Jeff Alden

Published by
Cowbridge Record Society
1 Mill Park, Cowbridge, CF71 7BG

Printed by
Keith Brown and Sons Ltd
55 Eastgate, Cowbridge

ISBN 0 9537029 2 8

PREFACE

This book is once again the product of the enthusiasm of the members of the class in Local History which I took for the Cardiff University Centre for Lifelong Learning, in Cowbridge in 1999.

As with *Cowbridge: Buildings and People*, we have endeavoured to find out as much as possible of the history of many of the older houses of Llanblethian. Our initial sources of information were the 1840 tithe apportionment and the censuses from 1851 to 1891; we have also studied rating lists, land tax assessments and family deeds which were deposited at the Glamorgan Record Office, to whose staff we are indebted for their help. At Cardiff Central Library, we have made extensive use of the notebooks of David Jones of Wallington, and we are very grateful to the Librarian for permission to use extracts in this book. The staff of Bridgend Park Street Local Studies Library, also unfailingly helpful, have made available to us copies of the *Glamorgan Gazette* and other local material; similarly the staff of Swansea Library have allowed us to inspect issues of *The Cambrian*.

A most useful source of information was *Llanblethian in 1895 - A Boyhood Walk* by Robert Thomas, and we are very pleased that Mr Derek Thomas, the copyright holder, has given us permission to include extracts from this booklet. In addition, our thanks go to those residents of Llanblethian and Cowbridge - including Becky Jenkins, Joyce Tonkin, Vivienne Whythe, Mervyn Harkett, Ronnie Harris, Walter Stone and Connie and Bill Taylor - whose lively reminiscences help to bring the history of the village to life.

We also wish to thank all those Llanblethian residents who kindly made their property deeds available to us, and showed us around their homes. Despite all this, there are some omissions - and for some properties it has proved well-nigh impossible to draw out a coherent account in the time available. More research remains to be done.

Thanks are also due to Keith and Eurion Brown for their great help in seeing this book - and the others we have published - through the production process.

Even though we have been able to go into more detail than we could do in the Cowbridge book, for many properties we have more information than could be printed. Certainly because of the considerable contact between Llanblethian and Cowbridge, some further information can be found in *Cowbridge: Buildings and People* and its Source Book. For those who wish to find out more, our 'sources and references' file will be deposited in major libraries (including Cowbridge, Park Street Bridgend, Cardiff Central, Glamorgan Record Office, National Library of Wales). Readers may also contact the Cowbridge Record Society for information.

Jeff Alden

CONTENTS

LLANBLETHIAN: AN INTRODUCTION

This attractive and much sought-after village in the heart of the Vale of Glamorgan has a long history of settlement. Tumuli - burial mounds - dating from the Bronze Age dot the plateau to the west of the village, around *Breach* and *Marlborough* farms. Llanblethian Hill is the site of an extensive Iron Age camp, *Caer Dynnaf*; the ditches and walls of this large multivallate fort are still clearly visible.

The village itself is built on the valley slopes running down to the river Thaw and its tributary valley of the Factory brook. It became the centre of the Norman manor of Llanblethian, and it is a source of local pride that the village existed long before Cowbridge was created as a new town within the manor in the thirteenth century. The church, *St Quentin's Castle* and various field patterns, reflecting the strip cultivation of the three-field system of farming, are of Norman origin.

In the medieval manor, we know of the existence of a fulling mill, of wind- and water-powered grain mills, and we also know the names of many of the tenants, and the names then used for some of the fields. It was an extensive manor, stretching north far beyond Llanblethian village to include Trerhyngyll and Aberthin, with an economy based on farming, and with a system of inheritance whereby property passed on to the youngest son.

In the eighteenth century, Llanblethian had few large houses, but was essentially a village of farmers, labourers and craftsmen with some emphasis on weaving. A century later, it had started attracting more wealthy residents, including retired military and naval officers on half pay. Newspaper advertisements of the time show that among the attractions of the village were the availability of hunting in the neighbourhood, and its proximity to the town of Cowbridge - and to coal for investment purposes a few miles to the north.

Among the families drawn in to the village were a number from Rochdale in Lancashire, especially the Entwisles and Royds. Although a great deal is now known about these families, their other residences, their family interconnections and their role in the social life of the Vale of

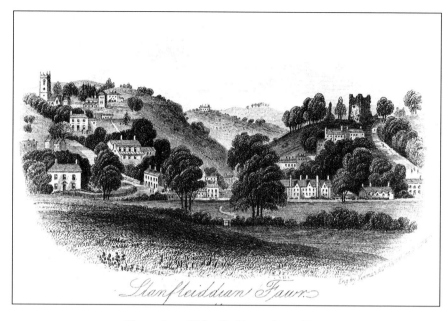

Engraving of Llanblethian, about 1875

Glamorgan, we still do not know why they chose Llanblethian as their home. The Entwisles and Royds owned property here from 1822 onwards; many other gentry families were attracted to some of the larger houses as annual tenants. Such were, for example, Sir Robert Blosse in *Great House*, or John Sterling, who started his career as a *Times* correspondent from a house somewhere in Llanblethian.

At that time, however, most of the people of the village were not well-off, and some were relatively poor. Maltsters, weavers, carpenters and other craftsmen, farm labourers and servant men and women made up the majority of the population. These included in-migrants from the West Country and west Wales, attracted by the higher wages paid in the Vale of Glamorgan, at a time when local people were being drawn to work in the coalfield to the north. Few owned their own homes, and many had little security of tenure - short-term leases being common - or security of income, especially in farming where many were hired at the annual fairs. The lord of the manor in the nineteenth century was the Marquess of Bute.

Llanblethian continued to be very much a workaday village until the mid-twentieth century, when changes in employment patterns, in car ownership and in society in general saw the gradual arrival of a large number of incomers who lived here but worked elsewhere.

★ ★ ★ ★ ★

In the following pages we have attempted to describe something of the history of many (but not all) of the older properties within the village and on the plateau to the west. The book follows a route through Llanblethian, starting near the church and then meandering through the village in a pattern which can be followed on the map on the next page. This walk ends at the foot of Broadway Hill, near the river bridge; then two properties near *Cross Inn* - the inn itself, and *Pentwyn*, are considered, and the book concludes with a study of the three significant buildings in the west of the old parish - *Crossways*, *Marlborough* and *Breach*.

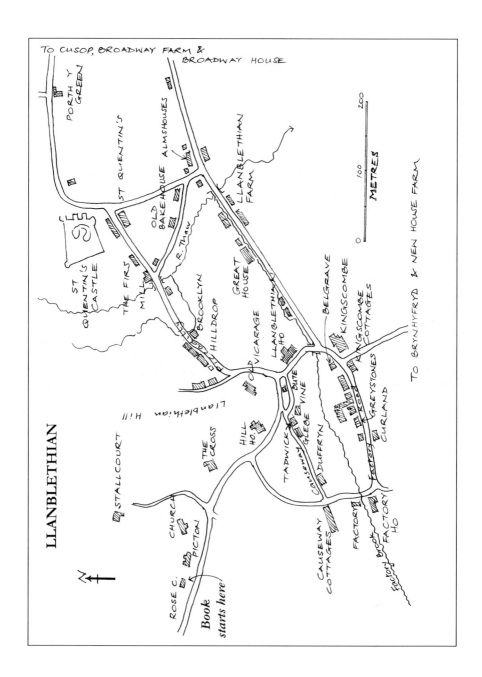

1: NEAR THE CHURCH

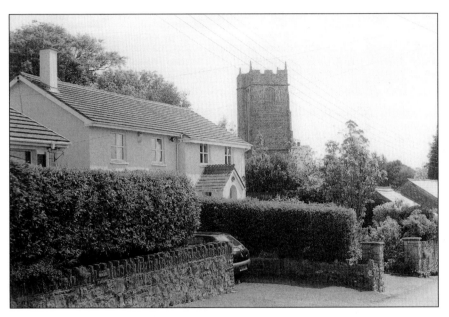

Rose Cottage and the Church

It is difficult to believe that **Rose Cottage**, now modernised and extended, was once a 'squatter's cottage', built on land which was regarded as waste but which belonged to the manor of Llanblethian. The builder was a Llewellyn, probably Edward, the son of David Llewellyn who is recorded in 1824 as being the tenant of an adjoining garden, also the property of the Marquess of Bute.

In a Royal Commission enquiry on land in 1893, Edward's grandson, another Edward Llewellyn, a carpenter of St Fagans, stated that his grandfather built the house about 1830, 'on the strength of a promise from the Bute estate officials that a lease in perpetuity be granted him at a rent of a shilling a year'. The outbuildings - stable, cart shed, cowshed - were added, bit by bit, as he could afford them; the total cost was about £10. The land carried a right of common (to allow animals to graze) on the waste land of the manor.

Edward Llewellyn senior, born in Llanblethian in 1788, a farmer of fifteen acres, was the occupant in 1840 and also in 1851 with his Caerphilly-born wife Jane, and three children, David, Jane and Elizabeth. He is probably the Neddy Llewellyn who is said to have recited a poem in the *Picton* next door, about the 1840 seance and 'ghosts' in *Great House*. He died in 1859. The next recorded tenant is his married daughter Elizabeth, with her husband, Thomas Richards, now farming only ten acres. Elizabeth however died in 1870, and so the house reverted to another Elizabeth Llewellyn, a widow, who had probably been the wife of David Llewellyn, recorded as the son of the house in 1851. (Thomas Richards moved on to farm the much bigger *Stallcourt* farm nearby). This Elizabeth Llewellyn had six children, including the carpenter Edward mentioned above, and farmed twenty-one acres on the Downs, and, according to Edward's evidence, some glebe land in the village.

The key point of Edward's evidence to the Royal Commission, however, was that his mother and her family were evicted from their cottage in October 1880. At this time all squatters' premises in the manor of Llanblethian had been offered for sale. The Bute agents offered Mrs Llewellyn eighty shillings (£4) for the house, which she refused. According to Edward, the house was in 'a very good state – the best in the village as a cottage'. Revaluation by the estate office raised the offer to £5, which she also declined; sadly she was then forcibly evicted 'on to the road by bailiffs accompanied by a policeman. When informed she must take 100 shillings or nothing, she accepted.' Fortunately at the end of that day, her cousin took pity on her and gave her accommodation.

The house was subsequently let to David Jenkins (at eight shillings rent per year), thus ending the Llewellyns' fifty-year occupancy. By 1891, he had been followed by John and Mary Williams. After a sequence of tenants, *Rose Cottage* was once again occupied by Llewellyns from the 1930s on.

Next door to *Rose Cottage* is **Picton House**. The Llanblethian tithe map of 1840 records a terrace of three dwellings here under the ownership of James Hiscocks, a Cowbridge grocer apparently then living in the village. We know that Hiscocks had owned the cottages in 1824 as the Bute estate 'terrier' (land inventory) of that year showed 'the garden in front of his cottages' belonging to the Bute estate. It is possible that these cottages, like *Rose Cottage*, were 'taken in from the waste' of the manor of Llanblethian somewhat earlier.

In 1840, the cottage nearest to the church was occupied by Elizabeth Jones, then came the house and garden of Mary Lloyd and at the west end of the terrace was an inn and garden also in the occupation of Mary Lloyd. She is named as an innkeeper of Llanblethian in 1819, and is still recorded as living at the *General Picton* in 1844, but not in the census seven years later. The notebook of David Jones of Wallington, the celebrated Vale of Glamorgan historian of the nineteenth century, states:

> In Molly Llwyd's time, dancing took place for two or three nights at the Picton. Outside the Picton there was a pabill (pavilion) for dancing in. It was a rudely-built structure, posts, with wattled sides, and thatched. The young people would meet twice or thrice a week for dancing. The paraphernalia of the Morris Dancers was kept in this pabill, Morris dancing being then quite a recognised public amusement, and frequent exhibitions of it were made about the country. The pabill at Llanblethian was accidentally burned down.

The choice of the *General Picton* as the name of a Llanblethian public house remains something of a mystery. The general was from Carmarthen, but his elder brother (who had changed his name to Turberville) lived at Ewenny Priory. Hopkin James in *Old Cowbridge* stated that it was thought that the great general was driven from Ewenny Priory by a Cowbridge coachman when he set out for Waterloo. Local pride and victory fever possibly account for the name.

The original building continued in multiple occupation until late in the twentieth century. The 1851 and 1861 censuses show John Williams, a victualler and farm bailiff from Llantwit Major, as head of household with his wife Frances. Christopher Evans, an agricultural labourer, and his wife lived next door. David Jones commented:

> Dancing for some years has been discontinued and the revel (initially at the Whitsun Fair, and later on Easter Monday) has sunk into a mere carousal. Our host John o' the Picton emulates his neighbour Shon y Gwaith (in the King's Head) as to who shall have the best tap, and the competition for that honour causes each of them to add an extra bushel

of malt to his brewing, to gratify the village topers. The thing is probably finished up with a little fighting, at least it is a portion of the standing annual gossip of the village to enquire after the event 'Has there been any fighting?' The General Picton is by far the best house of the two. Close to the church, it derives all the benefit that bell-ringing, marriages and burials can bring it, as well as being the place of meeting for all parish vestries.

An article in the *Central Glamorgan Gazette* on 18 June 1869 emphasised the importance of the inn for village affairs:

The 32nd anniversary of the Loyal St Quintins Lodge of the Manchester order of Oddfellows took place at the General Picton Inn last Saturday. Members, headed by the Cowbridge band, proceeded to the Parish Church for a powerful and eloquent sermon by Revd Thomas Edmondes, then processed to Cross Inn and through Westgate into Cowbridge to the Town Hall for refreshments; then up Eastgate and over Broadway to their lodge room for dinner.

In 1871, Thomas Morgan, born in St Hilary, was the innkeeper - he lived in the *Picton* with his wife and niece, and Margaret Jenkins, a widow, lived in the adjoining property. By the time of the 1881 census, the *Picton* had been taken over by Edwin Thomas and his family, and Margaret Jenkins was still living next door. Edwin Thomas and his then larger family, together with four lodgers, was in the *Picton* in 1891, while Margaret Jenkins continued at the age of eighty-eight to live in the attached dwelling, but was then accompanied by her nephew Harry Sedgebeer, his wife and son. Kelly's directory for 1895 puts Henry Sedgebeer as landlord of the *Picton*; in 1906 it names Mrs Mary Morgan, and in 1911 Mrs Elizabeth LA Morgan.

Ownership of the building had passed on the death of James Hiscocks in 1858 to Anne John, his late wife's niece, who died intestate in 1860. Her three brothers had assumed the name Jones and all emigrated to the United States. By a conveyance of 1870, Simon Lloyd Jones 'of 244 California Street in the city of San Francisco in the state of California', the surviving brother, sold to John Morgan, farmer of Llanharry, for £300 'that dwellinghouse and public house known by the name and sign of *General Picton* and also a dwellinghouse or cottage adjoining with the brewhouse, stable, pig styes and gardens to the said dwellinghouse situate near the

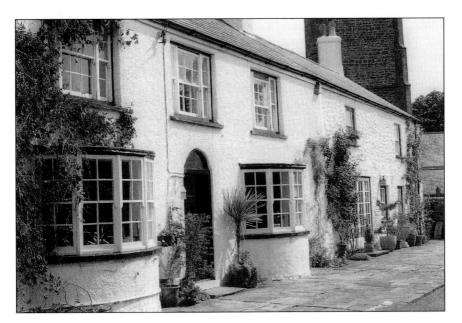

Picton House

church, used as a public house now in the occupation of Thomas Morgan, and the dwelling house or cottage adjoining of Margaret Jenkin, widow.'

John Morgan and his family sold the property in 1896 to Mrs Margaret Davies of Barry, from whom it passed in 1913 to Mrs G Yorath, the last of the absentee landlords. She in turn conveyed the building in the following year to James Edward Llewellyn (who died in 1922) and his wife Elizabeth, during whose ownership the public house ceased trading.

Elizabeth Llewellyn died in 1931. *Picton Inn*, as it was still called, passed to Miss Edith Llewellyn with *Glen View*, the centre and eastern sections, being bought by Sidney and Mrs Emily Llewellyn. Three years later *Picton House*, the former *Picton Inn*, was sold to Edgar Chedzoy and his wife Lilian, whose two daughters Brenda and Lilian were born here.

The Chedzoy sisters confirm that during the years 1934 to 1949 there were still separate entrances to the three cottages, and no interconnecting links. Two paths led to *Picton House*, one directly in front of the main entrance – the window above having been opened up by their father – and the other beside the outhouses. They had electricity in one room, and one cold water tap in the back kitchen. Members of the Llewellyn family occupied the other two cottages, the middle section comprising one room up, one room down, a kitchen and a staircase. In the back garden was a privy for each family, a three-seater for the Llewellyns and a two-seater for the Chedzoys. Their father had closed up the well but there was a spring in the back cellar, requiring constant baling out.

In March 1962, Edgar Chedzoy sold *Picton House* to Dr Bernard Knight, forensic scientist. Dr Knight's ownership lasted only until October of that year, but must have made such an impression that he has used the nom-de-plume Bernard Picton for his subsequent detective novels.

The **Church**, dedicated to St John the Baptist, is a grade I listed building. The earliest part is the north window in the chancel, dating from the twelfth century - which is the date of the earliest mention of the church, in a charter which shows it being made a possession of Tewkesbury Abbey. Until 1994, *Llanblethian church* was the mother church of the parish of Llanblethian with Cowbridge, and the vicar of Llanblethian at one time also had oversight of other churches, including Llansannor and Welsh St Donats. Today it is a church within the enlarged parish of Cowbridge.

The fine Somerset-style tower, like that of St John's, Cardiff, was reputedly the gift of Lady Anne Neville, heiress to the lordship of Glamorgan, and wife of Richard, Duke of Gloucester, later to be King Richard III (who is also supposed to be the donor of the Llanquian aisle in Cowbridge church).

The interior was heavily restored by CB Fowler, the diocesan architect, in the 1890s, the plaster being removed so that the grey limestone and dark mortar pointing dominates. However, restoration did expose the fine oak roof - though much of the medieval timber has had to be replaced. The Norman tub-shaped font is carved out of local Sutton stone. Other features of interest inside the church include the oak reredos in the chancel (the work of William Clark of Llandaff in 1911), the pulpit carved out of Penarth alabaster, Forest of Dean red sandstone and Bridgend Quarella limestone, some sepulchral slabs in the tower, and a thirteenth-century stone effigy of a man, with a greyhound at his feet, in the side chapel/vestry. Among the wall memorials, that to the parents of Sir Leoline Jenkins, the 'second founder' of Cowbridge Grammar School and of Jesus College Oxford, is worthy of attention, as is the Entwisle memorial, and the benefactions board.

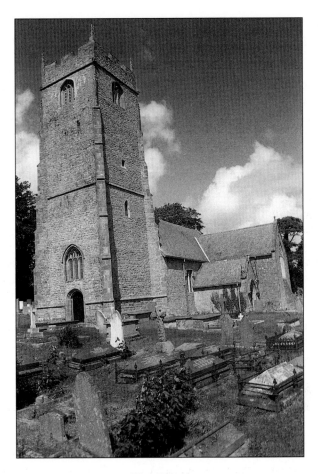

The Church

When the crypt under the vestry was opened up during Fowler's restoration, it was found to contain the remains of about 200 bodies. Whether the crypt had been an ossuary for bones removed from the churchyard, or the burial place of people killed in Owain Glyndwr's rebellion, is a matter of guesswork.

The south porch is clearly later than the main body of the church, and is offset slightly to the west of the south door. Its exterior is fine ashlar, of

Sutton stone (quarried near Southerndown), with some worn but interesting gargoyles, and there are some noteworthy memorial stones inside the porch.

The tower contains a ring of six bells, cast originally by the Evans brothers of Chepstow, and Rudhall of Gloucester. They were restored and rehung in 1994. One of the bells was a gift of Sir Leoline Jenkins, and two were given by his brother Evan Jenkins, income from whose Charity contributes greatly to the maintenance of the church.

There is a long list of the names of the clergy who served the church and parish. The first known vicar was 'Thomas, Vic de Llanblethian et decanus' in 1208, who was followed in 1217 by Magister Radulph Maelog. In 1231, Eustace, a monk who had been sent by Tewkesbury Abbey, was ostracized and 'harshly used' by the local people, and was only saved by the threat of excommunication upon the parishioners.

Around the corner from the church, on the upper slopes of Llanblethian Hill and just under the Iron Age fort, is **Stallcourt House**. This, as it stands today, was built in the late nineteenth century by WA James of Cowbridge, who built several substantial houses in and around the town, all of dressed stone. These included *St Crispin* and *The Shield* in Eastgate, and *Stafford House* in Westgate, where James himself lived. *Stallcourt* has changed little in appearance since its construction. It is square in shape, and consists of four large square rooms downstairs, of identical measurement, two on each side of a corridor.

The house was constructed close to the original site of *Stallcourt Farm* which was initially part of the Caercady Estate. Caercady House near Welsh St Donats was the home of the Jenkins and Thomas families, and so we see various Jenkinses and Thomases among the owners of *Stallcourt*, until its sale to John Homfray of the Penllyn estate in 1879. It remained a Penllyn property until the 1960s.

In 1792, the farm was occupied by Thomas James, yeoman, who leased it from Lewis Jenkins. James died in that year, and left the property to his wife Mary; she soon married a widower of some substance, Rees Adam, who hailed from Llanharry. Adam extended the size of his farm by renting other lands in Llanblethian, but died in 1815, after falling from his horse near *Cowbridge Town Mill*.

A second sad occurrence linked to the mill was the death in 1823 of Twm Thomas, a butcher who then lived in *Stallcourt*. Being somewhat

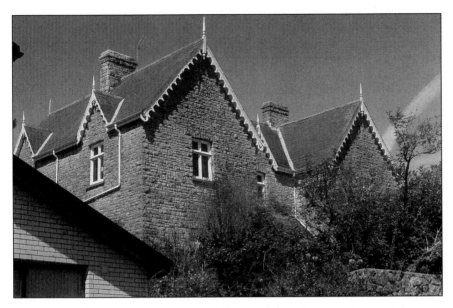

Stallcourt

under the influence of drink, he stumbled and fell into a watercourse near the mill – from a bridge whose side walls had been destroyed. 'A peaceable and inoffensive man, he lost his life due to the inefficiency of the parish officers . . .' wrote David Jones of Wallington.

Richard Griffiths occupied the farm at least between 1840 and 1861. In the 1851 census, he is recorded as having been born in Cadoxton, Neath, in about 1797; his wife Mary was born in Llanblethian. Richard farmed sixty-three acres, with the assistance of two labourers. Also in the house was their general servant, Matthew Harry, from Pyle, and two lodgers, boys from Aberdare – Gwilym and Gomer Williams. Mary died in 1852, and Richard's second wife in 1858. In 1861, Richard lived here with his son Richard, aged seven, but, sadly, young Richard died soon after enumeration day; his father died in 1867.

In the 1871 census *Stallcourt* was lived in by Thomas Richards, a forty-year-old farmer and widower who farmed ninety-two acres and who with his wife Elizabeth had moved here from *Rose Cottage* near the *General Picton Inn*. Two general servants were employed to help him with his young family of two sons and two daughters.

Henry Jones, from Llysworney, was here in 1881, farming fifty-two acres. His wife, Elizabeth, was born in Llanblethian. They employed a general domestic, and had three lodgers at the house - the Revd Owen Bowen, curate of Llanblethian, who came from Myddfai, Edward Henry Boyle, a tutor-teacher from Norfolk, and Robert Leonard, a sixteen-year-old scholar born in Clifton, Bristol.

Jones, however, had moved to *Breach* by 1884, and in 1885 the farm was occupied by David Thomas, aged forty-five, who in that year was brutally murdered on Llanblethian Hill. He and two of his brothers had left Penyrheol farm in Llysworney over twenty years earlier, to seek their fortune in America, in the coal-mining area of Pennsylvania. David in particular succeeded in making money and then returned to the Vale of Glamorgan and settled at *Stallcourt*. He was renowned as a shrewd cattle dealer and generally esteemed in the district as 'of genial, good tempered bearing'. On the night of 30 October, after celebrating a successful day's sales with a drink or two in the *Duke of Wellington* in Cowbridge, he was waylaid on his way home up Llanblethian Hill, killed with a billhook and robbed of his money. The murderer was David Roberts, a former soldier who lived with his father, Edward, in a small cottage in Piccadilly. The money was discovered hidden in the cottage; Roberts was found guilty of the murder and hanged at Cardiff prison on 2 March 1886. David Thomas left a wife and four children.

Anna, his widow, remained at *Stallcourt*. In the 1891 census, she was recorded as being forty-six years of age, from Pembrokeshire. Her three children lived with her - Jane, born at Llysworney, and Thomas and Mary Elizabeth, both born at Llantrisant. Revd Thomas Cynon Davies, from Llandysul, Cardiganshire, also lodged here. Anna ran the farm with some help from Thurstan Bassett of *Crossways,* and from her son-in-law, Fred Williams, who was very involved in the horse-racing world and bought hunters for the Glamorgan Hunt. He became landlord of *The Bear* hotel in Cowbridge in 1926.

Thomas Thomas, the son, returned from farming in Penllyn to take over the tenancy of *Stallcourt* in 1916, and farmed here until 1926. It is now a private house.

The Cross is named after the medieval preaching cross (grade II listed) which stands on the green outside the house, where, it is claimed, the Llanblethian 'pleasure fair' was held up to the mid-nineteenth century. 'It

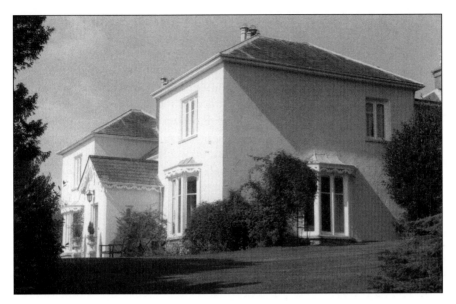

The Cross

was held annually from time immemorial on the green on Easter Monday, when the village and neighbouring lads and lasses assembled for physical and social pleasure, dancing to the music of such primitive instruments as the tin whistle or concertina, and regaling themselves with the simple refreshments of the time, provided by elderly dames of the village', wrote EW Miles, the Cowbridge solicitor and historian, in 1923.

Originally a cottage, *The Cross* had two wings added during the nineteenth century - the right-hand one in the mid-nineteenth century and the left towards 1900. These were built to accommodate the increasing number of residents at the house, and perhaps because of the increasing wealth of the occupiers. Today, both wings are joined by a front porchway, which provides a spacious inner hall. The rear of the right wing has an unusually steep and narrow staircase leading to a number of small rooms, with low ceilings, which were originally servants' quarters. A large room downstairs balances the lounge in the left wing and overlooks the lawns and shrubs of the extensive gardens, previously cultivated by Lady Byass during her stay here during the second world war. The house is on rising ground and has pleasing views over the village and countryside.

The field *Tair Erw wrth yr Eglwys* ('Three Acres beside the Church') in which *The Cross* was built, was land belonging to the Carne family in the late sixteenth century. It eventually passed to Rees Adam of *Stallcourt*, who sold off the lower part, of about one acre, to Joseph Thomas, a gardener of Llanblethian, who converted it into a garden. In the deed relating to this sale, the lane at the bottom of the garden is referred to as *'Heol Gristly'*. Thomas sold the land in 1806 to John Rowland, and it is Rowland who built the first house on this site. He quickly sold it to Sarah Morgan, of Eglwysilan, and later of Leach Castle near Bonvilston and of Llancarfan. An early tenant of the Morgans was Molly Evans, earlier a servant to the Trahernes of St Hilary, and the mother of Hester Kennedy, who married Revd Browne Williams of Llanmihangel and moved in gentry circles.

The mortgaged house was sold to Robert Nicholl of Dimlands, Llantwit Major, in 1818, and by him to the Rochdale-born William Royds who was then living in *St Quentin's House*. It seems to have been a property investment for Captain Royds, as different occupants are recorded - John David and others in 1831, Anne Lewis in 1840, Ellen Traherne (Royds's niece) in 1849.

According to the 1851 census, *The Cross* was then occupied by Edward Hodges, a widower, and family. He was a schoolmaster, employed at the National (or Church) School established in 1839 on the Cardiff Road in Cowbridge. He was born in Mevagissey, Cornwall, and had three young children, John, Edward and Elizabeth.

A deed of 1853 stated that the house was in the occupation of Nathaniel Plimer, an artist-decorator, and Miss Margaret Entwisle. Plimer had earlier done some work ('painting, papering and colouring') for Revd JM Traherne at Coedriglan, and was probably working for Margaret Entwisle who became the owner in 1854, and who also employed the architect David Vaughan: this may well have been when one wing was added. Margaret was another of the Rochdale people who had come to Llanblethian in the nineteenth century, and had lived with her brother Robert in *Crossways* before moving to *The Cross*.

On the death of Margaret Entwisle in 1870, the property passed to her great-niece, Frances Traherne, the youngest daughter of Revd George Traherne of St Hilary. She moved into the house with her mother, Mrs Ellen Traherne, née Royds, also born in Rochdale, and who had lived in *The Cross* in 1849. Frances died in 1872; her heir was her brother, Revd

George Montgomery Traherne of St Hilary, who conveyed *The Cross* to John Homfray of the Penllyn estate in 1879, the year Ellen Traherne died.

In 1881 the house was occupied by John Watkin Phillips, physician, who was born in Wrington, Somerset. He was aged fifty and lived here with his wife, Mary (from Llantwit Major) and their nine-year-old son, Arthur. Dr Phillips used a pony and trap to transport him to visit patients and employed a groom named Stephen Hitchcock, and four general domestic servants. He moved from *The Cross* to High Street, Cowbridge, and thence to *St Crispin*, Eastgate, in 1894.

Frederick Dunn had moved into *The Cross* by 1884. In the 1891 census he is described as a mining engineer, aged forty-six, born in Carmarthen. With him were his wife, Harriet, his six children, a governess and three servants. Frederick Dunn was a leading citizen in the area and a county magistrate for the Cowbridge Petty Sessional Division. The Dunns were the nearest to the popular conception of the 'lord and lady of the manor' in Llanblethian at this time. On the Investiture of the Prince of Wales in 1911, for example, it was recorded in the parish magazine that:

> Mr and Mrs Dunn very generously entertained all the children of Llanblethian to an excellent tea on the lawn at The Cross. After tea, sports were provided and the successful competitors received useful prizes. The rest of the evening was passed in listening to selections on the gramophone. As the children left The Cross, Mrs Dunn presented each child with an Investiture souvenir in the form of a beautifully designed box of butterscotch which we feel sure each recipient values.

Frederick Dunn died in 1911 and his wife in 1915. They are both buried in Llanblethian churchyard. The boys were all keen cricketers, and members of the Cowbridge cricket team. Tragically, three out of the five Dunn brothers did not survive the first world war. Frederick EP Dunn, however, continued to serve Cowbridge Cricket Club for many years as a player, secretary and president, and the memorial gates at the entrance to the Athletic Club grounds are a permanent tribute to his memory. He died in 1959, aged seventy-seven.

By 1923, *The Cross* was the home of William Brabazon Hallowes, JP, a Glamorgan magistrate for the Cowbridge Petty Sessional Division.

During the second world war, the house was occupied by Lady Byass (a member of the Gonzalez Byass sherry family), who had moved from Llandough Castle when it was taken over by the army. She was said to be a formidable person with a piercing voice. Every Sunday morning she would insist on being taken by pony and trap to Llandough church where she played the organ (much to the dismay of the local congregation as her playing was somewhat discordant!).

Hill House stands further down the hill from *The Cross*. A substantial house, it appears to have been extended at least twice from the original building, which has the date 1726 inscribed on one of the massive walls. The wide hallway leads to the centrally-placed stairs, with well-proportioned rooms on either side. The verandah is of Victorian date. The fine gardens have been well described in an early Joanna Trollope novel.

We are almost sure that this was one of the properties owned by Thomas Wilkins of *Great House* in the early eighteenth century, and after his death by his son Cann Wilkins. William Thomas, a land agent and property owner, lived here in 1775, when it was sold by him to Thomas Lewis of Cowbridge, together with the stable, barn and rickyard on the western side of the road (now converted into a separate house).

In 1791, Revd Robert Nicholl of Llanmaes bought the house (and Thomas Lewis's furniture in it), but after four years sold it on to Revd John Morgan, the vicar of Llanmaes. On his death, it passed to his widow, Mary, and then to a niece, Ann Thomas, who lived in *Hill House* from 1824 to after 1840. Some of her letters, to Mrs Jones of Bath (formerly of *Crossways*) have been preserved, and give a picture of life in the village in the 1830s - vandalism linked to drinking at *The Picton*, buying a mare at St Mary Hill fair, the availability of coal from a depot at The Golden Mile inn, and in 1836 - 'my house is full of workmen painting and papering, the walls had gone so shabby'.

By 1851, *Hill House* was occupied by William Edmondes, together with his wife, sister-in-law and three servants. He was described in *Hunt's Directory* of 1848 as solicitor, town clerk, clerk to the guardians of the Bridgend Union, and superintendent registrar. According to David Jones of Wallington, he shot himself in a house (now demolished) in Church Street, Cowbridge, in 1855, having embezzled £1200 from the Bridgend Union. There was a great deal of local sympathy for his widow, and a fund was set up by Robert Nicholl-Carne to support her.

The next inhabitants were William Smyth, a lieutenant in the Third Inniskilling Guards, and his wife Ann (from Llandow) and daughter. Walter Smyth, their son, became a chemist in Merthyr Tydfil; his first wife died in

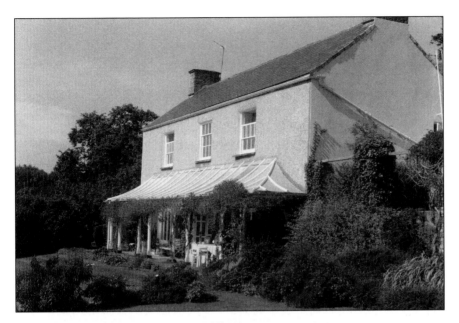

Hill House

childbirth in 1855, but he remarried Mary Annie Morgan of Llanblethian in 1866.

From 1870 to 1892 William Thomas, of a Vale farming family, and his wife Jane, from Merthyr, and three children lived here, having moved from *Cowbridge Town Mill*. William Thomas was a maltster and manure dealer, and his sons were in business with him. He owned the malthouse in Factory Road until it was taken over by Hancocks Brewery. William Thomas died in 1892; his son, William Richard Thomas, who married Elizabeth Rogers (daughter of the Cowbridge ironmonger who, by coincidence, had shot himself in 1882), took over the property.

On her husband's death in 1900, Elizabeth continued to live in *Hill House*, until after her remarriage, when she became Mrs Moon. She sold the house to Thomas Thomas of Red Farm, Penllyn, (son of David Thomas of *Stallcourt*) who was building up his holdings in Llanblethian, in 1908, when the tenants were George Morris and his wife, who had previously lived in *St Quentin's House*.

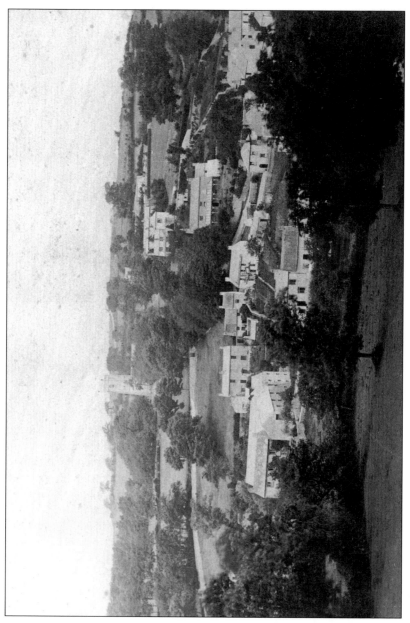

Llanblethian in about 1895

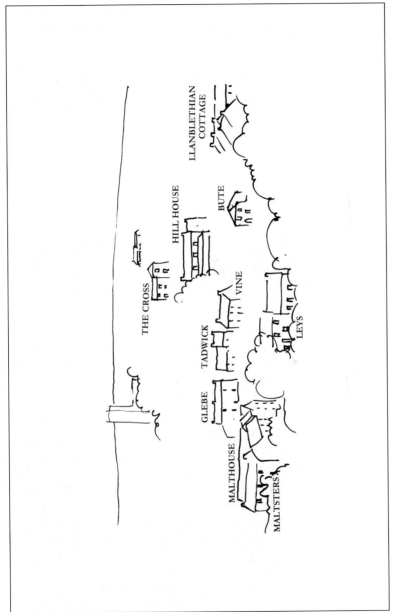

Llanblethian in about 1895

THE CROSS

HILL HOUSE

GLEBE

TADWICK

VINE

BUTE

LEYS

LLANBLETHIAN COTTAGE

MALTHOUSE

MALTSTERS

29

Joseph William Hall was the occupant of *Hill House* in 1914. He was a hay dealer, and a Glamorgan magistrate; his wife was reputedly a member of the Bird's Custard family. In 1926, Francis William Crawshay lived here.

2: THE CAUSEWAY AND FACTORY ROAD

Tilla Bach is the name traditionally given to the lane now called The Causeway, leading from Church Hill to *Causeway Cottages*. The fields to the north of the lane - now occupied by relatively modern houses - were known as *Erw Mr Carne* and *Tri Chwarter Broynog*, and the history of the ownership and occupancy of these fields is well documented. To the south of the road, the land sloping down to Factory brook was mainly glebe land, the property of the church. The old thatched houses along Tilla Bach were grouped at the Church Hill end: *Bute Cottage*, *Vine Cottage*, *Tadwick* and *Glebe*, with *Duffryn* on its own at the west.

Bute Cottage, listed in the Bute estate 'terrier' of 1824, was then a cottage leased to James Bradley of Cowbridge. The lease had been taken over by Gervase Turberville of *Llanblethian Cottage* opposite by 1840, and was then in the tithe apportionment described as 'stable and yard' - perhaps erroneously, for in 1851 James Reynolds lived here (and was recorded here in 1852, 1871 and 1874). James Reynolds was the enumerator of the 1851 census in Llanblethian. Initially a tailor, he became a property owner and auctioneer; he was treasurer of the Cowbridge Wesleyan chapel, and a member of the Oddfellows. Another claim to fame is that he was five-times married.

The bungalow named *Pleasant View* stands today on the site of **Vine Cottage.** This was the home around 1800 of Captain Christopher Hancorne, among whose forebears were vicars of Llandow and St Donats, and the Hancornes of Pitt in Gower. In 1840, *Vine Cottage* was owned by John Williams, a Llanblethian mason who also owned the adjoining properties, and was occupied by Revd Robert Phelps, vicar of Penllyn, who had married Hancorne's daughter Mary. Phelps died in Swansea in 1850 'in the street, of liquor' as *The Cambrian* put it.

Then followed a fairly rapid sequence of residents. As far as we can tell, John Webb, born in Sully and a painter, lived in *Vine Cottage* in 1851 with his wife, three sons and one grandson. In the following year, Jenkin

William occupied the house. Edward Llewellyn was here in 1861 and Daniel Jones in 1871 and, when the house was put up for sale in 1878, Thomas Mordecai was the occupier. Three years later, Thomas's widow Joan, a laundress, was still here with her two daughters, also laundresses, a son and a grandson. By 1910, Edward David, a direct descendant of the owner of 1840, lived here with his brother and sister, but by 1926 the house was in ruins. Edgar Chedzoy, then of *The Picton*, was responsible for its demolition and replacement with *Pleasant View*, and moved in during 1962.

Less is known about **Tadwick**, formerly called *The Homestead*, than about the houses on either side of it. In the mid-nineteenth century it too was owned by John Williams, and was occupied in 1851/2 by John Jenkins, a Bonvilston-born coachman and his family. It is likely that Thomas Morgans, a fifty-three-year-old labourer born in Llanblethian, occupied the house in 1861 (his son David was then a sixteen-year-old wool weaver). Morgans was recorded living in Tilla Bach in 1871 and 1881, probably in the same house. Ernest Chedzoy and his family, including Edgar who built *Pleasant View*, were in *The Homestead* in 1910, and were responsible for raising the roof of the cottage; the former roof line can still be seen on the wall facing the lane. The Chedzoys bought the house in 1923.

There are some fine architectural features in **Glebe**, described by the Royal Commission as of seventeenth-century date. Its dressed stone windows with square heads and sunk-chamfered mullions, its stone stairs with a cross-slab roof, and its back-to-back fireplaces and chimneys, make it one of Llanblethian's most interesting buildings.

Despite its name, there is no evidence that the house was part of the church lands, but probably took its name from the field adjoining it to the west, which was part of the church glebe. The house originally belonged to the Castlemynach estate; it was leased in 1730 by Richard Talbot of Hensol to Jenkin Evan, yeoman, of Llanblethian. It was then described as 'a cottage and garden in the occupation of Elizabeth Williams'. A subsequent lease, of 1777, between William, Earl Talbot and David William of Llanblethian, labourer, stated that it was then a 'ruinous cottage' - but the lease for three lives had as a condition that it was to be kept in good repair by the tenant.

John Williams the mason was considered to be the owner in the 1840 tithe apportionment, but he died in 1842 and ownership passed to his second son, David, who advertised *Glebe Cottage* for sale in 1878 - 'three beds, parlour, kitchen, back kitchen, dairy, pantry, stable and coach house, cistern, large garden, now occupied by Mr Llewellin Richards at £9 a year; subject to a life interest'. Llewellyn Richards was the son of Thomas Richards who had farmed *Stallcourt* in 1871; in 1881 he was a twenty-one-year-old farm labourer living in *Glebe* with his sister Jane and young brother Thomas. A deed of 1880, when David Williams of Aberthin, retired builder, mortgaged the property, quoted Benuel Edwards as the occupant - but as Edwards was also named as the occupant of a property in Factory Road, it can be assumed that he was the lessee and Llewellyn Richards a sub-tenant.

The sale was apparently not successful, and the house remained in the Williams family, with David's nephew, Thomas Williams, who was also a stonemason, occupying it in the 1890s. Robert Thomas in his review of Llanblethian in 1895, remembered Thomas Williams living in 'a very long house which had seen better days. When drunk, he indulged in bouts of crockery-smashing. For every dish he smashed his wife would do likewise'. Thomas Williams and his sister Ann Jones owned the house - and the two next-door cottages - in 1910.

At the end of the lane, **Duffryn** is a well-proportioned, slate-hung cottage. It was owned in 1840 by Thomas Bassett and occupied by John Williams; in 1851 Evan Millward, a huntsman born in Pentyrch, lived in the house, with his wife who came from Llantwit Major. All five children - three daughters and two sons, ranging in age from four to twenty-four - were born in Llantwit. Evan Morgan, a millwright, lived here in the early 1870s. Elizabeth Llewellyn, the widow who had been evicted from *Rose Cottage* by the Bute estate in 1880, was in *Duffryn* in 1881, with just two of her children. Henry Jones, who had earlier lived in *Stallcourt* and then *Breach Farm*, owned and occupied the house in 1910.

Causeway Cottages, forming a neat terrace of limestone-built and slate-roofed houses, look as if they were directly associated with the nearby woollen factory - but there is no evidence to support this. Since 1840, the owners (initially James Hiscocks, who also owned the *General Picton*, and then the Llewellyn family) have had no connection with the factory, and

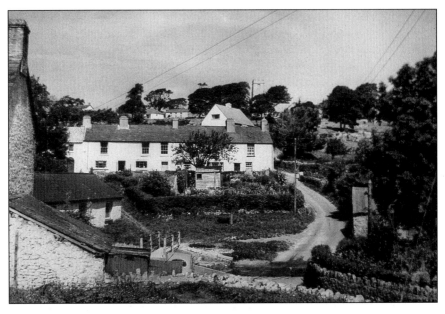

Causeway Cottages and the Woollen Factory, about 1950

not one of the recorded occupants since 1840 has been employed in the textile industry.

These have been essentially workers' cottages, with little continuity of occupation through the years. Robert Morgan, father and son, one a butcher and the other a huntsman, occupied two houses in 1851 and 1861; Robert the butcher, with a great capacity for enjoying himself, was also the father of William who occupied *Great House* in 1881, and the great-great-grandfather of David John the present-day Cowbridge ironmonger and agricultural merchant. The only other people throughout the nineteenth century who were here for consecutive censuses were William James, a stonemason from Llandow, and Thomas Williams, a mason from Cowbridge, both in 1881 and 1891.

Llanblethian's **Woollen Factory** was long celebrated for the production of cloth - 'flannel' used for shirts, dark blue serge, and suitings, black with thin white lines, and *brethyn llwyd*, a hard-wearing grey cloth. Much of this would be made up into clothes by the tailors of Cowbridge in the nineteenth century, but one inhabitant of the village, Becky Jenkins, still remembers ladies wearing tall black 'Welsh' hats - the cockle women of Penclawdd - coming to the factory to buy the black material with red stripes that they habitually wore. The factory, which contained two looms, was water-powered, and occupied the low building just across the stream from the house; it had ceased operation by 1913. The looms and millwheel are now at the Museum of Welsh Life at St Fagans.

Use of the factory for weaving is only documented from the 1830s, and up to the middle of the century weaving was essentially a domestic industry, with a number of houses in the village containing weaving looms. 'Johnny the Weaver', the landlord of the *King's Arms*, now *Belgrave House*, and Robert Thomas of what is now known as *The Old Bakehouse* - he was a handloom weaver employing seven men - were the best-known of the domestic weavers in 1851.

Factory House, and the adjoining building, have however had a much longer association with the production of woollen cloth. There is mention of a tucking mill or fulling mill - tucking was a process of shrinking and hammering material to consolidate it, and needed water power to drive the hammers - in Llanblethian from the fourteenth century onwards. Though the earlier deeds - such as the 1314 survey on the death of Gilbert de Clare, and the 1570 manorial survey which stated that 'Jankin William holds a fulling mill granted to Hugh Carne for 99 years from 1516' - do not precisely locate the mill, from later references it would appear that the fulling mill occupied the site of today's *Factory House*.

By 1782, the 'felt mill' was part of the Llanmihangel estate, leased to Edward Ballard of Cowbridge, but in 1804 the occupant was John Jenkin the younger of Llanblethian, tucker, who also had leased 'the croft, mill, pound house and garden' from Thomas Wyndham of Dunraven, as by then the Llanmihangel and Dunraven estates had combined.

The first named weaver here was William Price, also described as a woollen manufacturer. He was the son of another William Price, also a weaver, of Llantwit Major. The Llanblethian William probably had six children, including two pairs of twins; his daughter Margaret in 1838 married David Davies of Gelligaer, described on the marriage certificate as a musician, and known in south Wales as a celebrated harpist.

Price was followed in the factory about 1850 by Thomas Evans, born in Llandaff. He was a weaver, employing one man, probably his lodger,

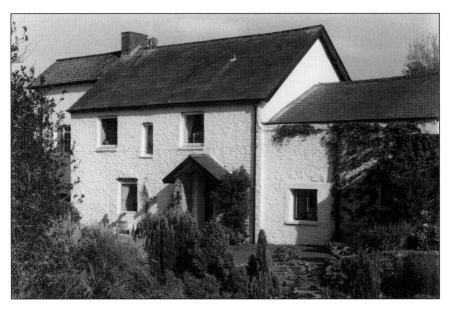

Factory House

Daniel Jones, a handloom weaver from Llysworney. Bradford James, who was the occupant from 1869 on, employed four people; subsequently Evan John, who manufactured 'all kinds of woollen goods, stocking yarns, etc', lived here for a short time, and then came David Jones, born in Llanfabon but who had moved to Llanblethian from Pentyrch.

The last of the woollen manufacturers was the Howells family. Charles Howells was born in Caerphilly, but had lived in Merthyr and Abercarn before settling in Llanblethian by 1885 with his Llantrithyd-born wife. Llanblethian churchwardens' accounts show that charity monies were used to aid the apprenticeship of Tudor Howells, his son, in 1886, and Tudor was working with his father in the factory at the time of the 1891 census. After his father's death, we assume that Tudor continued as a weaver, as his mother lived on in the house. It was she who entertained Princess Mary of Teck, later Queen Mary, who 'took tea in the garden' when on a tour of the Dunraven properties in south Wales.

Dunraven ownership ended in 1913 when the 'dwelling house (containing parlour, back kitchen, pantry with store room over, four bedrooms on first floor), woollen factory, stable for one horse, coach house, etc' was auctioned at *The Bear* in Cowbridge; the purchaser was William Jenkins of Llanblethian. From that date it has been a private house, though in the early years the Jenkinses had a sweetshop here.

The first house on the right along Factory Road has been known as **Curland** or the *Old Post Office*. In 1840 this was one of a number of properties owned by Thomas Bassett, and was occupied by David Richards, who in the 1851 census was described as a sixty-three-year-old farmer of twenty-six acres, employing one man. Two daughters, two sons, (all unmarried) and two grandchildren lived with him in the cottage. By 1861 he had increased the size of his farm to eighty acres, and his family to seven, mainly different ones from the previous census!

Bennett Edwards was recorded in the house in 1874 and in 1880; he too was a farmer, born in Cowbridge, who moved in 1881 to *Porth y Green*, at the top of Constitution Hill. It is not certain who lived in *Curland* between 1881 and 1895; but from that date to at least 1910 the occupant was Henry Williams. The house served as a post office for Llanblethian in the mid-twentieth century.

Westbury, opposite, had been a barn for many years but was converted towards the end of the nineteenth century into a cottage. Thomas Williams, who owned *Curland*, also owned *Westbury*, the occupants at the end of the century and at least until 1910 being David and Polly Williams.

Greystones, formerly *Rosedew*, is one of the properties which in the seventeenth and eighteenth centuries was used for weaving.

When David William, weaver of Llanblethian, died in 1701, the inventory of his goods suggested that he was not a wealthy man. The total value of his possessions was only £13. 2s. 6d - but this did include three weaver's looms, so he probably employed some other weavers in his cottage, which was placed conveniently close to the fulling mill where the woven cloth could be treated. David William also owned two houses, one of which was built on the site of *Greystones*. He bequeathed to his 'son, Edward David and his heirs for ever' the cottage and the croft (or plot of land) opposite - and this pairing of a cottage and $1^3/_4$ acres of pasture appears continuously in subsequent records.

By 1767, the property was described as being 'late of Ann David' - probably Edward's widow - but it was by then owned by William Thomas,

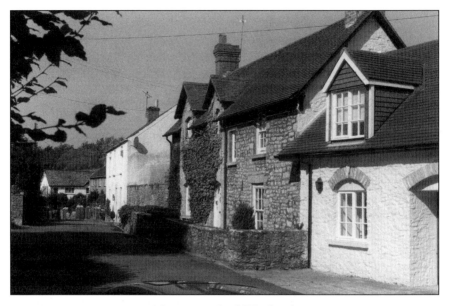

Greystones (and Westbury)

a land agent who seemed to be accumulating property in the village. It passed by inheritance, via Mary Jones, to Evan David of Fairwater, Cardiff, and then stayed in the possession of the David family throughout the nineteenth century.

John Jenkins was the occupier in 1840 of the 'dwelling house, barn and garden', with the narrow strip of field opposite - no mention of weaving now - and in 1851 he was described as a farmer of seventeen acres, born in Llanblethian, with his Cowbridge-born wife Ann and four daughters. One of these daughters, Gwenllian, married William Edmunds, a farmer from Llantrisant, and it is they who are shown in the house in 1861, having moved in soon after the death of her father in 1857.

Gwenllian died in 1868, and by 1871 Thomas Jenkins, a maltster, lived in *Greystones*. He had moved from the house next-door, now known as *Maltsters Cottage*, where his parents continued to live. It is likely that Jenkins worked in the malthouse which had recently been built; he also farmed ten acres, including the field across the road. Thomas and his wife Catherine, from Bettws, near Bridgend, brought up their family of five children in *Greystones*.

The tall, three-storey L-shaped malthouse dominates photographs of Factory Road at the end of the nineteenth century. It had been built around 1870 for William Thomas, who had been the miller at *Cowbridge Town Mill* and who moved to *Hill House*, Llanblethian. The malthouse dwarfed **Maltsters Cottage**, where the inhabitants from at least 1840 to 1871 were John and Ann Jenkins - confusingly, the same names as the inhabitants of *Greystones*. This Ann, however, had been born in Llanblethian. She is recorded as living on in the house after her husband's death, until at least 1891; her brother, Richard Morgan, lived with her, as he had done since 1851.

Windsor House is an early twentieth-century building, erected by Edward Llewellyn, probably the man whose mother was evicted from *Rose Cottage* by the Bute estate in 1880.

At various times in the past, up to three cottages existed on the site of **Leys Cottage**, but in the mid-eighteenth century, there was one cottage here, leased to Jenkin Butler by the Carnes of Nash Manor. After Jenkin's death, his widow Catherine continued living here but, from 1798 to 1807, the Butler lease having expired, a fresh lease was granted to William Bowen.

Bowen was replaced as tenant by William Hardee, who appears (with some variations in the spelling of his name) to have lived in the house until the mid-nineteenth century. Certainly, the tithe apportionment of 1840 records William Hardee in the house and, in the churchwardens' accounts of 1851, William Hardee is one of the 'industrious poor' of the parish. However, the census of that year records the name of the occupant as William Hardin, an eighty-eight-year-old coal-carrier, born in Newton Nottage, with his wife Catherine, aged fifty-five, and son Thomas, aged fourteen.

The Cambrian newspaper records the death of William Harding aged 93 in 1854 (presumably the same man, despite the slight discrepancy in age) and by 1861 William's widow Catherine, described as a nurse, who had been born in Llantwit Major, lived in what then was one of three cottages on the site. Gwenllian Roberts, a widow born in Llantrisant, and James Braddick, a coachman from Stockland in Devon, and who subsequently moved to *The Firs* near *Llanblethian Mill*, were the other occupants.

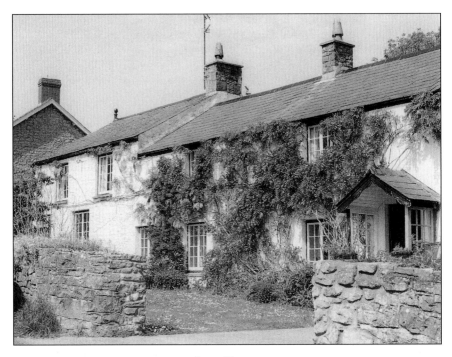

Leys Cottage

By this time the annual Llanblethian pleasure fair had ceased to exist on the land near the church and cross, but a modified version continued as Kitty Harding's fair, held here in her cottage. EW Miles wrote:

> I remember being taken to her fair by a nurse from the village on one occasion. Her cottage had a capacious hearth, with stone seats on each side under the chimney which were appropriated by the older boys, while cracking jokes and nuts, and consuming the small but primitive luxuries sold at the table at the side of the room.

After Catherine's death it is difficult to work out who lived in the cottages, though it is likely that one was occupied by William Jenkins, a farm bailiff from Colwinston, and his family. Ownership changed from the Carnes to Revd JCF Morson, headmaster of Cowbridge Grammar School, and then to Edward Llewellyn who also bought the adjoining property, where he built *Windsor House*.

In 1891, the three cottages were occupied by the Barbers, Thomases and Boobyers. Mr Barber, who worked at *Marlborough Grange*, was away at the time of the census; his wife was described as a charwoman. The children had been born in Cirencester and Llanfair Discoed, Monmouthshire, so the family had certainly moved about the country. The son, though crippled, could play the piano with his feet. The middle cottage was occupied by Isaac Thomas, a carpenter who had been born in the *Bakehouse* in Llanblethian (and one of whose sons was Robert who started the Cowbridge building firm which still exists). The Boobyers lived in the end cottage on the right. Aaron came from Stoke St Gregory in Somerset, Harriet from Pendoylan; she kept a sweet shop here.

By 1910, all had again changed; the three occupiers were then John Harding, Fred Bryant and Thomas Jenkins. In the mid-twentieth century, the Perch-Thomases, parents of Viv Whythe (now a resident of Cowbridge) bought two cottages and converted them into one, despite the different floor levels; the Georges moved into the third, and then bought the others to make one cottage.

Belgrave House was earlier known as the *King's Head* public house. The earliest record we have of the occupancy of the *King's Head* is the 1840 tithe map when John Thomas is shown as owner and occupier. In the 1851 census he was described as a publican and weaver, from the Swansea area, aged seventy-two, living here with his wife, Margaret, and their grandson, Thomas Jones.

John Thomas was the famous Siôn-y-Gwehydd, John the weaver, who helped to make the *King's Head* the village ale house. To quote David Jones of Wallington:

'Sion-y-Gwaith' is quite a household word at Llanblethian and popular enough to have conferred his name upon the little 'public' instead of the name the sign bears. If you wanted this house you may ask twenty people in the village for its whereabouts and not one of them at first thought could tell you anything of the King's Head, but ask for John the Weaver's and the youngest child could tell you.

John Thomas had three daughters, Ann, Sarah and Catherine. Ann had married James Kitt, a carpenter from Pinhoe in Devon and, though John Thomas still lived in the house, it is James who was regarded as the head of the household in 1861. John Thomas died intestate in 1866, and James and

Ann Kitt took over the property without reference to the two other sisters. Legal wrangling ensued until 1881 when the property was sold to Thomas Jones, the rural postman who lived in *Ar y Mynydd* near Piccadilly.

David Jones's diary for 7 May 1880 stated 'John the Weaver's old house all in ruins, and grass growing over the stones'; perhaps something of an over-statement, because the 1881 census records the Kitts as still living here. However, a new house, in typically solid late-Victorian style was erected on the site in the 1880s, and in 1889 Thomas Jones sold this property to David Williams of Aberthin.

In the census of 1891, the house, now called *Belgrave House*, was occupied by Elizabeth Williams, aged seventy-two, a lady of means, born in Llantrithyd. She was David Williams's widow, and in 1891 purchased the eastern triangular part of the garden from GW Nicholl of *Llanblethian House*. Sadly Eliza Williams died in July 1893, from injuries sustained when she was thrown out of her carriage; an inquest was held in *Great House*.

The next tenant was William Thomas, a carrier of goods from the railway at Cowbridge, followed by John Williams John. The property was bought in 1898 by Edward Llewellyn, the carpenter of Wenvoe, who went on to build *Windsor House*. The Llewellyns lived in *Belgrave* for some years in the early twentieth century.

Opposite *Belgrave House*, **Kingscombe Cottages** on the corner of Factory Road were probably built as one house, as the dividing wall is made of brick in an otherwise all-stone building. The western wall is six feet thick, and contained a bread oven as well as a large fireplace; the stonework suggests that this property dates back earlier than our records show.

It belonged to the Nicholls of *Llanblethian House* in 1840. Only one occupant, David Williams, was named in the tithe apportionment, but in 1851 there were two separate families here - that of Thomas Morgan, a forty-two-year-old farm labourer, born in Llanblethian, with his wife and nine children, and William David, a labourer on the roads, aged seventy-five, born in Swansea, together with three visitors. John Richards, a Llanblethian-born limeburner, replaced Morgan by 1852; he and William David were here in 1858, when the property was sold to James Giro of *Brynhyfryd*, and in 1861, when Richards is shown as having a wife and five daughters.

In 1871, the two families living in *Kingscombe Cottages* were the Lewises and the Davieses. William Lewis, a thirty-seven-year-old mason, was away

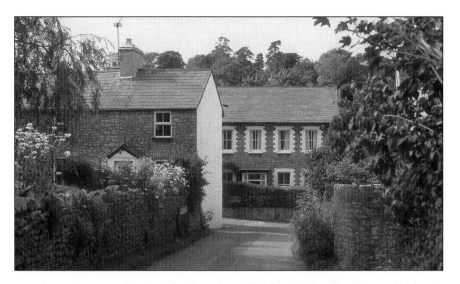

Kingscombe Cottages and Belgrave House

at the time of the census, but Margaret, his wife (born in Cowbridge) with four children and a lodger, lived in the corner house. Edwin Davies, a coachman, his wife Ann and eighty-year-old father-in-law David Williams (possibly the David Williams who lived here in 1840) lived in the other house. As Edwin Davies was born in Swansea, and the David/Davies surname was often confused, he could well have been a relative of the William David who lived here earlier.

After William Lewis died in 1884, Margaret earned some income as a laundress. Her son, a mason, and her daughter, also a laundress, lived with her in 1891, as did her uncle Thomas George, a pauper from Llandough. Edwin Davies's house was occupied by Joe Gifford and his family of five children in 1895; he was the son of Nathaniel Gifford who lived in a cottage (now demolished) in what is today the garden of *Llanblethian House*. By 1910, John Hopkins the stonemason was recorded as owner, having bought the property in 1901; David Davies (in the corner house) and James Tout were the occupants.

3: LLANMIHANGEL ROAD
AND 'THE LITTLE BRIDGE'

Up the hill to Llaned, the only house on the right was *Brynhyfryd*. An advertisement in *The Cambrian* in August 1839 stated:

> American Cottage - to be let or sold, with immediate possession, freehold beautiful romantic villa residence known as American Cottage. Five bedrooms, two parlours, hall, two kitchens, brewhouse, two-stall stable with hayloft, coachhouse, cowhouse with loft, and every convenience adapted to a house of this description; together with flower and kitchen gardens, shrubberies, etc. Apply JW Donne, Orange Street, Swansea.

This was *Brynhyfryd*, built, according to local lore, by an American; the owner, John Donne, was one of a Vale of Glamorgan farming family whose relations lived at that time in *Great House*. It would seem that the stable and outbuildings today form the core of the house called *Dulce Domum*.

Donne was initially unsuccessful in his advertisement, because the tithe apportionment of 1840 records him as the owner of an unoccupied property, and we have to wait until the census of 1851 for the first recorded occupier. Charles T Rhys, an attorney, and son of the noted schoolmaster of the *Eagle Academy* in Cowbridge, Thomas Rhys, married Jennet Meazey of Cowbridge in 1850, and they are shown as living in the house in 1851, with their servant. Charles Rhys was cut out of several wills at this time - leading one to wonder whether there had been severe family displeasure at his marriage.

The Rhyses moved to Tresilian on the coast near Llantwit Major, and were succeeded by the next census by James Giro and his daughter, Lita, and two servants. Giro was a widower, born in Gibraltar, and had a private income; he soon fitted into Cowbridge and Llanblethian society. The young Revd FW Edmondes records, for example, in his diary for 30 November 1867 'Dined at Mr Giro's - Lita's birthday, nineteen. Gave her prayer and hymn book', and in the following year . . . 'to dinner at

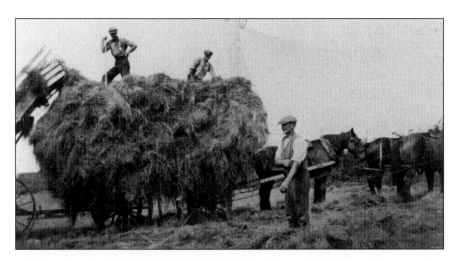

Haymaking at New House Farm, 1930s

Brynhyfryd'. James Giro died aged 72 in 1870, leaving the house to his elder daughter Sarah, who let the property, probably on an annual tenancy.

Giro was followed here by Revd M Vaughan, who did not stay very long, for in 1880 David Jones of Wallington recorded in his diary that 'Giro's house was empty'. By 1881, Eliza Roach, a widow from Brecon, lived here with her three sons, two nieces and a servant; in 1891, Harold Bird, a highway surveyor from Neath, was in *Brynhyfryd* with his wife and son – but they soon moved on to live in *St Quentin's House*. Harold Bird took over the ironmonger's shop which had been run by his brother Nathaniel in Cowbridge, and started the expansion of the business into the field now occupied by the garden centre.

Just above *Brynhyfryd*, a drive leads off the opposite side of the road to **New House Farm**, which was built, reputedly of stone from the 'Old Quarry' at the entrance to the drive, on land called 'Gibbs land'. This property in 1767 belonged to William Bruce of *Great House*, who had started building up his estate in Llanblethian in the 1750s. It passed by the early years of the nineteenth century to William Nicholl, a member of the land-owning family based in Adamsdown, Cardiff and The Ham, Llantwit Major, who leased out the farm. Tenants included Anthony Harding in 1851, and then Thomas David, born in Welsh St Donats, with his wife

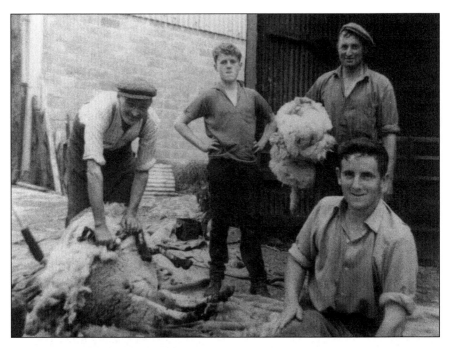

Sheep shearing at New House Farm, 1960s

Rebecca and daughter Elizabeth, who stayed in *New House* from the late 1850s to at least 1885. At this time, the farm land consisted only of three fields, of about twelve acres, but must have been farmed intensively, as David described himself as 'farmer and gardener' in 1871. By 1889, Thomas Thomas was in occupation as a dairy farmer; he was the eldest son of Robert Thomas of the *Old Bakehouse*. His wife Margaret was from Llantwit Major, and they had one son and three daughters.

Thomases dominate the pattern in the twentieth century. Hopkin Thomas was the tenant in 1910 and 1914 (when the farm was sold as part of the Ham estate), and from 1926 Barry and Mary Thomas, and then their son John Thomas and his wife Mary, owned the farm and lived here. When it was sold in 1967 (to Norman Thomas, the son of Sir Percy Thomas, the architect of the Severn Bridge and many other distinguished buildings) the farm was a successful dairy unit, with a total area of thirty-eight acres; sheep had also been kept. The house is now a private residence.

Back down the hill, past the fields which contain strip lynchets or ancient field boundaries, is **Kingscombe Farm,** one of Llanblethian's few grade II listed buildings. The front, facing up the hill, has stucco over local limestone and, though the porch is modern, has retained most of its Georgian character.

Although known as *Kingscombe Farm* this property, as described in the tithe schedule of 1840, consisted only of a house and garden with an Upper Field and Lower Field (both meadowland) totalling just over eight acres. It was owned, under the system of copyhold tenure according to the custom of the manor of Llanblethian, by William Lewis. He had inherited it, together with the farms of *Trebettyn* and *Llanquian Uchaf* (or *Hollybush*), both in the north of the parish, from David William of Llanblethian, who had purchased *Kingscombe* in 1807 for £974 from Andrew Armstrong of *Great House*. David William died intestate in 1827 and twenty-four-year-old William Lewis, born in Llanblethian, was his customary heir. By 1834 Lewis was married to a Swansea-born girl, Anne, and lived in Llanllwch near Carmarthen where their first son, John, was born. By 1835 the family

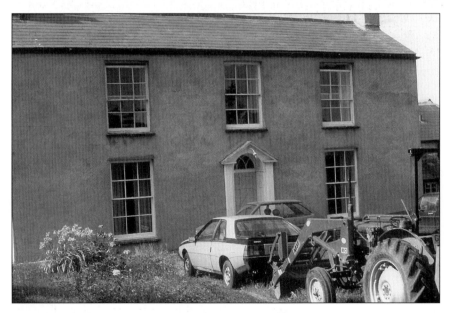

Kingscombe Farm, 1991

had moved to Earlswood Cottage, Cadoxton-juxta-Neath, where David, twins Catherine and Mary, and Gwilym were born. *Kingscombe* in 1837 was tenanted by John Williams, a surveyor of taxes, but at the time of the tithe schedule in 1840 it was apparently occupied by William Lewis, although his family was probably still living at Cadoxton where Gwilym was baptised in September 1840.

In the 1851 census *Kingscombe* was empty and William Lewis was living at *Hollybush Farm* on Stalling Down, describing himself as a farmer of 104 acres, employing four men; he was also a landed proprietor. Four years later he had died at the age of fifty-three; his widow Anne lived on until 1876 but not at *Hollybush*. Both were buried in Llanblethian churchyard although Anne Lewis died at Newcastle, Bridgend.

Her tenant at *Kingscombe* in 1861 was Georgiana Royds, a widow born in Ardwick, Lancashire, and her daughter Alicia Vittoria Royds. The two ladies were supported by a married couple, Joseph and Jane Strange, as domestic servant and cook, and two other servants. Georgiana was the niece of Sir Robert Peel, and the widow of Colonel William Royds of Rochdale, who had lived in Llanblethian in the 1830s, and who owned property in the village. He had died in Cheltenham in 1858, and she returned to Llanblethian to be near her son, Frederick Royds, who was living at *St Quentin's House*. Alicia went on to marry William Oldham, then of *St Quentin's*, in 1863; Georgiana died at *St Quentin's* in 1864.

In the 1871 census, *Kingscombe* again appeared to be vacant but the Miles family (including Ebenezer William Miles, then a solicitor's clerk) is recorded occupying the house during the year. In 1874, David Williams, a builder, who later retired to Aberthin, was a tenant for a short time, but by 1881 Arthur Treharne, a retired naval officer and his wife, Harriet, were in occupation. In 1886 *Kingscombe* was sold by the Lewis heirs to William Rees, an innkeeper of Graig Ddu, Dinas, who was living here as a dairy farmer in 1891 with his wife Anne, a niece, Bronwen Walters, and a maidservant.

A small parcel of land, on which the Sunday school (later the parish hall) was built, was sold to Llanblethian church in 1888; the rest of the land and the property was conveyed to Thomas Thomas, farmer, of Wern Fawr in Ystradowen parish, in 1895. David Jenkins, and then his son Richard, farmed here in the early twentieth century.

Becky Jenkins, still a resident of Llanblethian, remembers that when she went in 1923 at the age of fourteen to work for Dick Jenkins in the farmhouse, the building was subdivided. A Mrs Bassett, with her son and a daughter who taught at the Girls' High School, rented the front room, the front stairs and two bedrooms. The invalid Mrs Jenkins senior lived in the other front room, and Dick and his young daughter in the back of the house. Dick's sister Martha came in from Factory Road to make the butter, 30 lbs at a time. Dick Jenkins kept his horses in the fields above Factory Road.

Almost opposite the parish hall, Factory brook makes a right-angled bend around two cottages, **Brook Cottage** and **Ger y nant**. The course of the river, and the difference in water level between the little bridge and *Great House* suggest that a mill once stood here - perhaps the 'little mill' referred to in a 1637 deed describing Factory brook as 'the river leading from the tucking mill to the little mill'. The buildings were part of the *Great House* estate conveyed to Major Andrew Armstrong of Llandough Castle in 1803, and ownership remained linked with *Great House* for much of the nineteenth century. In 1840, the tenant of one cottage here was Martha Thomas, but by 1851 there were two cottages, the westernmost one of which (today's *Brook Cottage*) was occupied by Gwenllian George, from Llantrisant. Initially described as a charwoman, she became known as a washerwoman and then a 'knitting woman', before moving to the almshouses further down the road by 1881. Of the other tenants, only Joseph Davies, a wheelwright born in Bedwas - who lived in the other cottage, with his wife and four children - stayed any length of time, being recorded here in both 1871 and 1881.

Just across the little bridge over the Factory brook, **Llanblethian House** is a fine late-eighteenth-century grade II listed building; a medieval stone doorway in the wall adjoining the road might well mark the site of an earlier property. It was known as 'the Nicholls' house' throughout the nineteenth century. Edward Nicholl, one of the Nicholl family of The Ham in Llantwit Major, and whose brother lived for a short time in *Hill House*, owned *Llanblethian House* in the first part of that century, and lived here for some of the time. The left-hand side was probably the servants' quarters, while the right-hand side, for the resident family, contained taller and more spacious rooms. At a number of times in the past - as at present - the house has been divided into two properties.

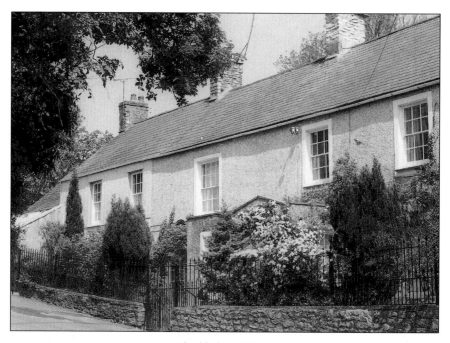

Llanblethian House

In the 1830s, it seems that Revd Thomas Powell and his wife lived here. He was from Brecknockshire, was curate of Llanmihangel with Flemingston, and had married the daughter of Captain McGregor of *Great House*. They had lived briefly at Llanmihangel and then moved to Llanblethian, where to supplement their income (and to support their family of seven children) they took in lady and gentlemen boarders. Thomas also taught at the Grammar School. His wife was of failing health; it was deemed noteworthy for a neighbour to write 'Mrs Powell is enabled to ride out in her phaeton, whenever the weather will permit her strong enough to walk across her drawing room with a stick.'

The paying guests in 1839, according to David Jones of Wallington, were Thomas Donne and his third wife, a wealthy English lady, and her daughter. (His first wife had been a farmer's daughter, and the second was Mary Anne Entwisle, the widow of Philip Entwisle from Rochdale). The Donnes however soon moved in with Thomas Donne's brother at *Great House*.

The 1851 census shows the three Powell brothers living in *Llanblethian House*. Thomas was then a widower, as was Revd John Powell, rector of Llanharry. John was the brother-in-law of Edward Ballard, junior, of Cowbridge, for John Powell and Edward Ballard had married the Thomas sisters of *The Cross* in High Street in Cowbridge, though Mrs Powell had died before John moved to Llanblethian. David Powell, the third brother, was a retired excise officer.

Something of a surprise occurred in 1856, with the marriage of Elizabeth, one of Thomas's daughters, to Revd Michael Farrar, second master at the Grammar School. He was a widower, she was a minor - the difference in their ages must have caused some talk! Eventually his son (who was therefore her step-son) married one of her sisters. Michael Farrar became headmaster of a school in Brecknockshire, but when Revd Thomas Powell died, the Farrars and some of Powell's sons emigrated to Canada.

The Powells were followed in *Llanblethian House* by the Ords. Ralph Ord died in Llanblethian in 1860, and the 1861 census shows his widow, Christiana, living here with four daughters, three sons and a servant. Mrs Ord had been born in north London, but the children had been born in Durham, Yorkshire, London and St Mellons, showing that the family had travelled a great deal. Four of the Ord children died between the ages of seventeen and twenty-seven while living in Llanblethian, and one more, aged twenty-five, after the family had moved to Eastgate in Cowbridge in 1868.

George Whitlock Nicholl, born in Roath, with his wife, three sons and three daughters, then came to live in the family home. The censuses for 1871, 1881 and 1891 all show GW Nicholl in residence, and during his occupation one of the rooms had its ceiling raised to accommodate an organ. The Nicholl estate was put up for auction at *The Bear* in Cowbridge in 1899. The house, with stables, coach house, lawns and gardens, was bought by DW Savours of Fontygary, as were the two cottages to the north, and the ruined cottage to the south, all of which would have been inside the boundaries of the two present *Llanblethian House* properties.

Just up the hill, and approached by a curving drive, stands **The Old Vicarage**, a large and solid house, which was built in 1900. In the porch can be read the exhortations *Pax intrantibus, salus exeuntibus* (Peace to those who enter, health to those who leave). The house in fact served as the

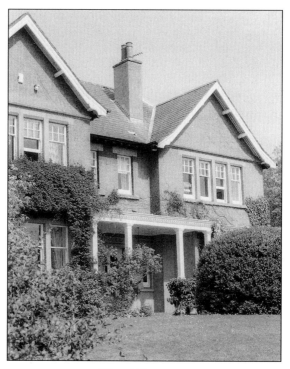

The Old Vicarage

vicarage for Llanblethian for only about half a century, and was built on the site of the even larger *Llanblethian Cottage*, which had extensive terraced gardens on the hillside above the house, and stables and coach house to the west (now the *Old Coach House*).

In 1822, Hugh Entwisle, one of a number of Lancastrians living in the parish in the early nineteenth century, bought *Llanblethian Cottage*. Hugh was the second son of John Entwisle, of Foxholes, Rochdale, and had entered the navy as a midshipman in 1795, serving first on the Amethyst; he saw action at Trafalgar, and was decorated. He was made lieutenant in 1806; his subsequent ships were the Pauline, Warspite, Bucephalus, Seahorse and Madagascar, from which he retired on half-pay in 1816.

Why he moved to south Wales is not known – but his father stayed (and died in 1818) at Cadoxton Lodge in the Vale of Neath, and had earlier been recorded as a regular visitor to Swansea for 'the season'. Hugh was then living at Drymma, near Neath. His father left him £5,500 in his will and, on selling Drymma (and Cadoxton), he moved, initially to Clemenstone in Llandow and then to *Llanblethian Cottage*. His account book showed that he extended the building, altering the front, building or re-building the verandah, and building the stables. His brother Robert and sister Margaret probably lived in the *Cottage* at this time, before moving to *Crossways*, but the wedding announcement of Hugh Entwisle and Mary Anne Royds in Rochdale in 1823 stated that he was 'of *Llanblethian Cottage*'. Captain Royds, father of Mary Ann, must have also lived here for some time, as an announcement in *The Cambrian* of 1829 lists the 'elegant and well-preserved furniture' of Captain Royds, to be sold as he was moving from *Llanblethian Cottage* to Bath.

By the time Hugh and his wife moved (to *Marlborough Grange)* in 1838, the house was described in the sale advertisement as:

> the compact and convenient residence of Hugh Entwisle in the pretty village of Llanblethian, consisting of dining and drawing rooms, hall, cellars, kitchen, back kitchen, larder, pantry, laundry, shoe room, etc. Four bedrooms, dressing room and water closet, two servants rooms and attics, four-stall and two-stall stables, saddle room, coach house, gig house, cow house, granary and pig styes, two gardens and orchard well stocked with good trees in full bearing, the whole enclosed within a wall and free from intrusion.

Gervase Turberville, Lt-Colonel in the 12th Foot (the East Suffolks) and a nephew of General Picton of Napoleonic Wars fame, is listed as owner and occupier here in the 1840 tithe apportionment. He married Elizabeth Dowell of Bath in the same year, but she died at Tresilian in 1844. He remarried the following year, and by 1849, after the death of his brother, had moved to the family seat at Ewenny. He was followed in *Llanblethian Cottage* by Birt Jenner, a retired captain in the East India Company, the youngest son of Robert Jenner of Wenvoe Castle. Jenner had a substantial household, with six servants in 1851 (including the mysteriously-named Charlotte Robitanski) to look after his wife and two children. Revd FW Edmondes records dinners and dances 'at Capt Jenner's', and even after the death of Birt Jenner in 1863, Mrs Jenner continued to entertain – in August 1865, 'Mrs Jenner had thirty to lunch after cottage garden show (in *St Quentin's Castle*) – very good spread'.

The next significant occupant was Morgan Joseph, a colliery proprietor who was born in Merthyr Tydfil, and who was here from 1875 with his wife and three daughters. His wife died in 1881, and Joseph had moved by 1884.

1884 saw the first use of the house as the vicarage for Llanblethian, when Revd JA Protheroe moved in (for the previous forty years, the incumbent had been Revd Thomas Edmondes, who lived in *Old Hall*, Cowbridge). By 1891 the property was vacant, probably becoming dilapidated, and the new vicarage was subsequently built on the site, the land having been presented to the parish by Frances Brereton, a daughter of Birt Jenner.

Among the vicars who have lived here were Revds Isaiah Roberts, Lemuel Hopkin James, the author of *Old Cowbridge* and *Hopciniaid Morganwg*, and Gilbert Williams. It is now a private residence.

4: PICCADILLY AND LLANBLETHIAN HILL

Photographs taken 100 years ago show a Piccadilly different from today in a number of respects: with more buildings, with thatched roofs, but smaller houses and hence many more people living here. The essential pattern of stone-built cottages and winding lanes was as true then as it is today, in this area set between the common land of Llanblethian Hill and the meadows around the river Thaw.

The two cottages on the lane running off Piccadilly at the foot of Llanblethian Hill are *Ar y Mynydd* and *Hillside*.

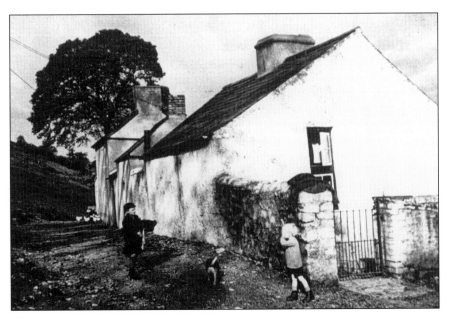

Ar y Mynydd and Hillside, 1936

In the early nineteenth century, *Ar y Mynydd* was the home of Richard Rees, nominally a mason but in reality a bit of a property developer. He was living here in 1819 when he mortgaged his properties; he was still here in 1840. It was then a much smaller cottage than *Ar y Mynydd* today – the house was considerably enlarged in the 1970s.

When Richard died in 1846, his widow Jane evidently found it necessary to convey the properties to Elizabeth Simkins, to whom they had been mortgaged. Five years later, the two adjoining cottages on 'The Hill' were both occupied by a John Rice and family, both gardeners, and both from around Swansea, probably father and son. Within a year, there was only one John Rice and also a John Webb living in Miss Simkins's houses: we are not sure who was where.

Ar y Mynydd was occupied in 1861 by a pauper widow called Ann Harding, and also by a journeyman tailor, the Devon-born James Tout and his wife Mary, who moved to various cottages in Llanblethian during their life.

Unoccupied in 1871, the 'cottage and pigstye with garden' was occupied by Morgan Morgan, shoemaker, for an annual rent of £5, when Philip Morgan became the owner in 1876. In 1881, Aaron Boobyer, miller, from Stoke St Mary in Somerset, whose brother had also moved into Piccadilly, lived in the house with his wife Harriet. They soon went on to live in part of *Leys Cottage*, and in 1891, Thomas Jones, a postman, lived in *Ar y Mynydd* with his family. Robert Thomas remembered Mrs Tom Jones as having a laundry, and the 1891 census records her daughter Elizabeth as being a laundress. Thomas Jones died in 1908. His obituary stated 'For many years he was familiar to the older inhabitants as a letter carrier in the district. As a faithful churchman, communicant, chorister and Sunday school scholar, the late Thomas Jones had few equals'.

By 1910 Richard David lived in the house; Thomas Williams of the adjacent *Hillside* was recorded as the owner. Soon after, the Harrises occupied *Ar y Mynydd*; they kept eight goats and cut fern from the common land on the hill for bedding. Jack Harris, sometimes helped by Fred Chissell, used to keep the paths there cut back, and burned the hillside regularly. It is a pity that no one is following in their footsteps, as bushes and shrubs have now spread all over the steep slopes. Jack Harris, who worked for Dick Jenkins of *Kingscombe*, used to shoot rabbits on Llanblethian Hill and sell them to the people of the village for Sunday dinner.

Hillside was another of the cottages owned by Richard Rees in the early years of the nineteenth century. Ann Evan was living here in 1819 when Rees mortgaged the cottage and his other properties in Piccadilly; she was also living here in 1834 when he took out a further mortgage from Elizabeth Simkins. Henrietta Perkins lived in the house in 1840.

In the late 1850s George and Ann Sandland moved from Broadway into *Hillside*. Sandland was described variously as a gamekeeper and market gardener and was born in Kingsbury in Warwickshire. He had married Ann Deakin in Lichfield in 1821. They had two daughters who died in infancy, and one son, and before moving to Llanblethian lived at Dyffryn Lodge, St Nicholas (presumably George Sandland had been employed at Dyffryn House). Ann died in 1867 aged seventy-one while George lived on in *Hillside* until 1874 when he died at the age of eighty-six.

A letter exists from Ann written in 1856 to her son Charles who had emigrated to Australia, having earlier kept a bookshop in Cowbridge. The letter is full of delightful village gossip, to do with St Nicholas rather than Llanblethian or Cowbridge. It mentions a surveyor's wife who had been committed to Cardiff prison for theft, a certain 'Harbottle' - a farmer at

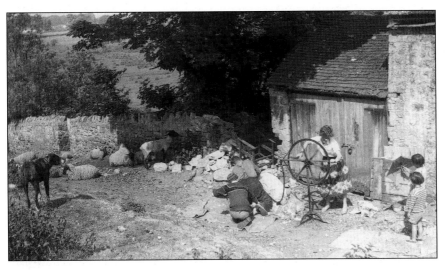

Sheep shearing outside Hillside, 1958: Herbert James with Billy and Pauline

Tinkinswood, who was dying from the effects of drink - and 'young Jane Edwards' who had been confined in something of an emergency in the parson's house shortly after a shotgun wedding. Ann also refers in graphic detail to the tragic explosion at Cymer colliery.

Charles was baptised at St Nicholas, lived in Dyffryn Lodge in 1841, and was educated at the *Eagle Academy* in Cowbridge. He died in 1909 in Victoria, Australia at the age of seventy-eight. He had become a farmer and had eight children. Some of his school books are still in the possession of his family.

After the death of George Sandland, Thomas Williams, another gardener, born near Taunton, moved into *Hillside*, and he bought the house in 1876. He mortgaged the property later in the same year, and a further mortgage in 1886 involved the interests of the Oriel family of Dowlais. Thomas Williams had married Ann Oriel, born on Caldey Island; two of their sons were Thomas Oriel Williams and Ben Oriel Williams, aged eleven and nine respectively in 1881, and there were five other children.

In 1895, Robert Thomas described the house as the village shop:

> Mr Thomas Williams lived there and he also kept a small farm and had the run of the hill for sheep. He also delivered coal. His wife was an invalid for many years. The shop catered well for the needs of the village. Could usually get what you needed, oil, soap, candles, sugar, flour and sweets. Easter Monday was a big day, usually ran a fair, at least that is what we called it, quite a lot of fun those days. Also, like my grandparents, they kept a donkey which was named Fanny. The donkey's name stuck and the family were identified by such.

In 1910, the owner and occupier was still Thomas Williams, but in 1927 the two sons - Thomas, living in Dowlais, and Ben, a tailor and outfitter in Port Talbot - passed on the property to their youngest sister, Rose Ellen, who had married Tom James of *Cross Inn*. Having grazing rights on Llanblethian Hill, the James family kept twenty sheep. Walter Stone of Llanblethian remembers: 'the Jameses in *Hillside* - Herbert, Tom, Ossie, Ralph, Dai, Frank, Idris and Ted. Most of them played cricket for Llanblethian, on the ground behind the Hunt stables, where Sir Sidney Byass had had a proper wicket laid for the Glamorgan Hunt XI to play against teams such as the Gentlemen of Ireland. Ted was a marvellous cricketer, a lovely bat'.

Hilldrop is one of the properties where the photograph shows that great changes have taken place: here stood, close together, two separate houses with different owners.

Where the garage stands today was a thatched cottage, which in 1713 was the dwelling house of Alexander William, who also owned *Brooklyn*. He left this house to his wife Joan for her life, and then to his son William.

By 1840, the owner was Revd John Williams, the grandson of Thomas Williams, the headmaster of Cowbridge Grammar School in the eighteenth century. John Williams was later described as 'of Wigginton Rectory, near Banbury in Oxfordshire, the eldest son and heir of Revd John Williams, late of Plaxtol in Kent'. Watercolours of Wigginton and Plaxtol, as well as Llanblethian, painted by Colonel WH Taynton, a relation of the Williamses, still exist.

The occupier here from 1840 to at least 1851 was Thomas Jenkin, a labourer on the roads, who received some poor relief as 'one of the industrious poor of the parish'. Thomas had been born in 1774 in Ewenny; his wife Ann was from Laleston. Isaac, his son, an agricultural labourer, had taken over the tenancy by 1861; he lived here with his wife, four daughters and two sons. The children had been born in Llanblethian, Marcross, Wick and Llandow, pointing out the temporary nature both of farm employment and of house rental.

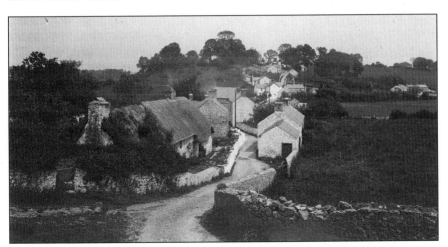

Piccadilly in 1905

The house was sold to William Thomas, the carpenter who lived in the house next door, in 1863, but was rapidly sold on to Richard Todd, a Cardiff shipbroker. When he died in 1872, his heir was Richard Rees Todd, who also owned *Brooklyn*. Throughout these changes of ownership, Isaac Jenkins, now described as a working maltster, continued living here. Three more children had been born by 1871, but four had left home, or died, and he had remarried.

Isaac and his wife were here alone in 1891. Robert Thomas described their home as being 'a small cottage with surrounding wall, well below the road. A stile leads down some steps to a yard in front of the house'. When Todd conveyed the property, along with *Brooklyn*, to George Williams in 1902, it was described as 'until recently occupied by Mary David, but now unoccupied', and by 1910 it was considered to be a garden - the cottage must have tumbled down. Walter Stone remembers it as 'a little cubby hole where some old boy lived'.

The history of *Hilldrop* proper has so far only been traced back to 1840, when the owner was Mary Thomas and the occupier Elizabeth Roberts. Elizabeth was still in the house in 1851 - a widow, she was described as a washerwoman, born in Coity - with her niece Elizabeth Rowland from Penllyn. Deeds show us that in 1863, William Thomas, a carpenter, lived here: apparently the William Henry Thomas, a carpenter and cabinet maker, from Mathry in Pembrokeshire, who is shown in the 1861 census as living in Piccadilly with his Llanblethian-born wife and son.

However, there was certainly a different William Thomas here in 1871, 1874 and 1881, and this William had also lived somewhere in Piccadilly in 1861. He was first described as a gardener, but by 1881 was a farm labourer. His wife was Catherine, his children Mary, Catherine and Evan. In 1878 the fifteen-year-old Evan was apprenticed to John Hopkin the stonemason of *Pentwyn*, and in the 1881 census he was regarded as a stonecutter. The Thomases were followed by George Mustoe, a general labourer, originally from Gloucester, and his family. Three of the five children had been born in Llanharry (one son, the twenty-seven-year-old Edward, was described as a collier, and so probably continued working in a pit to the north of the Vale).

At the turn of the century Benjamin Williams was both owner and occupier; he worked at Llandough Castle, and he and his wife were apparently devout Baptists. Early in the twentieth century, the cottage had a corrugated iron roof over the thatch.

The oldest deeds of property in Piccadilly which we have been able to find relate to **Brooklyn**, that 'messuage or cottage having to the north the road from *Llanblethian Mill* through the village of Llanblethian, and to the east the brook'.

Rees Nichol, a carpenter, was living in this house in 1713, when it was bequeathed by Alexander William in his will to his youngest son, also Alexander. In 1766, Alexander Williams, then of Holborn, London, and Mary Williams of Cowbridge, sold the house to John Lloyd of Cowbridge; the sitting tenant was a widow, Cissil Gibbon. Lloyd's grandson, a tailor named John David, conveyed the property in 1799 to Edward Rowland, a wheelwright of Llanblethian. Rowland sold off a piece of his garden to Thomas Jenkin, a cooper from the village, who then built a cottage here - now incorporated into the outbuildings of the modern *Coopersale House* next door. (This cottage was the home of David Roberts, the murderer of David Thomas of *Stallcourt* in 1885).

Rowland sold *Brooklyn* in 1839 to Arthur Malkin, one of the five sons of Benjamin Heath Malkin, the historian and topographer who lived at *Old Hall* in Cowbridge. BH Malkin, in addition to writing *The Scenery, Antiquities and Biography of South Wales*, also wrote *A Father's Memoirs of His Child,* telling of the brief life of Arthur's brother Thomas, who before he died at the age of six had written detailed stories about a fantasy land called Allestone.

Edward Rowland continued to live in the house despite the sale, as he is shown as the occupier in the 1840 tithe awards. Subsequent occupiers are not known until 1861, when the census records John Williams, a tailor born in Cowbridge, with his wife Harriet from Llanstephan, three sons and three daughters, living here. They had moved from *Causeway Cottages*. Ownership passed from the Malkins to Richard Rees Todd of Cardiff, who bought the house for £55 in 1863, but it remained the home of the Williamses until at least 1874, though by 1871 Harriet was a widow, living here with only her eleven-year-old daughter Mary Ann for company.

Thomas Jenkins, a stonemason, and his wife, three daughters and three sons, lived in *Brooklyn* in 1891, but when the house was sold to George Williams, a wheelwright of *Hillside*, in 1902, it was described as unoccupied. Williams also bought the garden opposite *The Firs* (at the bottom of St Quentin's Hill) and expanded his landholdings, so that by 1935 he was described as a farmer.

Opposite *Brooklyn*, **Rose Cottage** and **Half Moon Cottage** (both relatively recent names) were at one time home for five families.

Richard Rees bought this land when it was put up for auction in 1803 by the trustees of the estate of William Bruce of *Great House*. Initially he built two cottages; the **Rose Cottage** part was let first to Walter Hibbert and then to Catherine Richards. Rees sold this house in 1815 to Mary Williams, a widow, for £60.

Ownership can be traced using the deeds, so that we know that in 1856 the then owner Thomas Williams sold the house to Benjamin Price. He died in 1865; his heirs auctioned the property in 1868, and the successful bidder was John Howe. On Howe's death in 1881, the house was left in trust to his wife and daughters, and the trustees of his will conveyed *Rose Cottage* to Miss Mary Jones of *Llanblethian Farm* (niece of John Jones the tenant of the farm). By 1923 Mary had married Thomas Jones of Llantwit Major, and conveyed the property to Mrs Elizabeth Llewellyn of the *General Picton Inn*.

It is much more difficult to sort out the occupiers of the property, especially as tenancies were frequently for one year or less. In 1840, the tithe map shows William Roberts and Thomas Price living in *Rose Cottage*. The 1869 conveyance calls it a 'messuage converted into two messuages now or late in the occupation of Sarah Thomas'. We may make a fair guess that Jacob Jenkins and John Blethyn lived here in 1871; we are sure that Alice John and John Robert were in the house, as tenants of Howe, in 1874. A deed of 1897 saw the 'two cottages lately occupied by Mr Randall', but the 1891 census showed that there were two Randalls in Piccadilly. One, John Randall, a maltster's labourer from Somerset, lived with his family in a small, four-roomed cottage, which could well be part of today's *Rose Cottage*. If that is correct, the other half, only three rooms, was occupied by George Grittin, a stonemason from Hereford, and his wife.

Half Moon Cottage remained in the ownership of Richard Rees until the 1840s. In 1819 it was occupied by Jennet Lewis, widow, in 1834 by Mary Morgan and Jane Richards, and in 1840 by Mary Morgan, Thomas John and Ann John. By then it was evidently divided into three. Richard Rees's widow sold the house to Elizabeth Simkins in 1846, and in 1851 at least one of the subdivisions was lived in by Edward Evans, a cooper born in Llanwonno near Pontypridd, his wife Gwenllian and son Samuel.

On the death of Elizabeth Simkins in 1855, the house was left to her sister, Mary Shaftesbury Llewellyn, and subsequently to her nephew CT Rhys, the attorney, of *Brynhyfryd*. Mrs Jennet Rhys, his widow, was recorded as owner in 1867, and again in 1874 when one of the then two parts of the house was empty; the other was occupied by William Robert. Within two years, John Loader was paying £5 annual rent, and William Denbury £4 rent for the two parts, and the new owner was Philip Morgan, who sold the house in 1891 to WD Alexander, the retired miller of *Cowbridge Town Mill*. The occupants then were Jacob Jenkins, maltster labourer, and his children, and Isaac Williams, a blacksmith, and his family. It is possible that two rooms were occupied by Mary Wyatt, a charwoman, and her children.

Alexander is still recorded as the owner in 1910 when the occupants were Harriet Boobyer (formerly of *Ar y Mynydd* and *Leys Cottage* sweet shop) and Elizabeth Jones, both paying a rent of £5 a year. The property was then described as 'two very old freehold cottages and gardens in Piccadilly'.

Brook House, traditionally part of the *Great House* landholding, was between 1840 and 1851 occupied by William Jones, a thatcher who was originally from Coychurch. He was followed in 1852 by Rees Jones, a Llandow-born tailor, and his family. Mary, the widow of Rees Jones, was recorded in the house in the 1871 and 1881 censuses. In 1891, John Ralls, a carpenter born in Bridgwater, lived here with his family which included his son John, a solicitor's clerk, whose signature appears as witness to so many local house deeds of the early twentieth century. By 1910, David Spencer, one of the Spencer family of *The Mill*, owned and lived in the cottage, which stayed owned and occupied by the Spencers until the 1970s.

5: LLANBLETHIAN MILL
AND GREENFIELD WAY

For at least 475 years a water-powered corn mill has existed in Llanblethian. The 1570 manorial survey records its existence, dating back to a lease of 1526; then in 1582 and 1587 the then lord of the manor, the Earl of Pembroke, leased 'one water grist mill called **Llanblethian Mill**' firstly to Howell Meyrick and then to Thomas Williams, yeoman, of Llanblethian. Seventeenth-century deeds relating to the mill also exist - and also the sad details of an inquest in 1679 when Hopkin Rees, yeoman, was killed by the water wheel.

Revd David Nicholl of Llanblethian (possibly the father of Revd Henry Nichols, the first Sir Leoline Jenkins Missionary Fellow of Jesus College, Oxford, who served in the 'Welsh tract' of Pennsylvania in the early years of the eighteenth century) took an eighty-year lease in 1694, but the 1767 manorial rentals show William Bruce of *Great House* as the owner. A fuller account of the occupants starts with the sale of the mill, and *Cowbridge Town Mill*, by the Bruce trustees in 1796, to Henry Edmund, a Llanblethian farmer.

When Henry Edmund died in 1830, his will - leaving the mill initially to his wife Elizabeth - eventually gave rise to a large number of people having an interest in the property. However, in 1840 Elizabeth was recorded as owner and occupier, and by 1851 Edmund Edmund was installed as miller, living here with his wife Mary, two sons and two daughters. By 1861, he was regarded as a 'miller maltster'. In that year his son William, also a miller, married Gwenllian, the daughter of John Jenkins, a farmer living in *Greystones* in Factory Road, and by 1871 William was the resident miller.

When the mill was auctioned in 1877 (and sold to John Hopkins) it was described as 'house, mill, stable and pigstye in front of the mill, garden and orchard (where there were growing several walnut trees), croft or quillet of land which divides the river Thaw from the meadow called *Gwayn Beddor* (the field leading to *Cowbridge Mill*)'. The advertisement stated that 'the

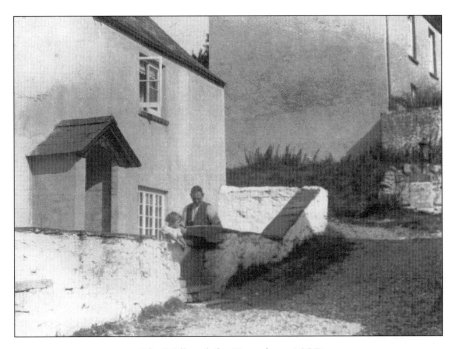

The Mill and the Firs, about 1927

machinery of the mill has recently undergone considerable improvement, a machine for refining flour has been added, and the large wheels are of iron'. William Edmund continued living here with his wife, three sons and three daughters but, by 1884, he had been replaced by David Spencer, born in Pendoylan, with his wife, three sons (David, Llewellyn and Gilead – the latter became a wheelwright in Bear Lane in Cowbridge) and their adopted daughter Emily Humphreys.

Llewellyn Spencer later ran the mill for a time, until at least 1920, but then it was taken over by Harry Stone, who lived here until 1954. Initially, flour was the main product. The mill contained refining machinery which, using a series of sieves and brushes, produced different grades of flour, and bran. The Stones also had a bakehouse on the other side of the road (where *Afon Ladrad* is today), and delivered bread (in competition with Thomas's bakehouse), to the villages around Cowbridge. They had a regular contract to supply the Grammar School with bread, and an intermittent one with the Girls' High School. Mrs Stone also kept a small shop in the building. At this time the mill was still owned by the Hopkins family, who had given the land for the *Baptist Sunday School*, and who kept horses in the walnut orchard.

Harry's son, Walter, helped keep the mill going until it was closed in 1948. Walter Stone states that closure happened after a visit from some local councillors with the River Board engineer, who explained that the sluice gates were contributing to the flooding of Cowbridge, and so Harry volunteered to close the mill and give up the water rights. By then the demand for milling had decreased considerably, however. The mainstay of the mill's production had become rough-crushed grain for cattle and chickens, and engineering developments meant that farmers could fix attachments, called kibblers, to their tractors to crush the grain themselves.

The *Mill* is now a private house, but the stones of the mill leat, which led to the mill wheel, are still in existence, buried in the garden.

The appearance of the rear of **Mill Cottage**, and the two stone staircases inside, suggest that it is of some age. It was owned in 1840 by Thomas Lloyd, from Rochdale, whose career seems to have been linked with the Entwisles. It was then just one cottage, occupied by William Keen, and in 1852 Thomas Cummins lived here. Between that date and 1861, it was probably subdivided, and the façade, showing the subdivision, possibly dates from this period. Cummins, an Irishman, and Mary Lloyd, a pauper weaver's widow from Penmark, were in the two parts in 1861; Mary's daughter Elizabeth, a schoolmistress, remained here for at least another ten years. Like many Llanblethian cottages, these had a variety of tenants, but some continuity was shown in the cottage nearer to the *Mill* between 1881 and 1891, when Joshua Thomas, a Carmarthen-born tailor lived here. Another Thomas, William - an older, Llanblethian-born labourer - is shown next-door in 1891 and 1895.

The first recorded lease for a cottage on the site of the **Old Bakehouse** is dated 1650; it was then owned by Howell Carne of Nash, and occupied by Mary William, a widow. The property stayed in the hands of the Carne family until the 1870s. By 1682, it was in ruins, but leased to Lewis William, a mason, who was probably responsible for the rebuilding. Subsequent occupants in the eighteenth century included Lewis Jenkin, a

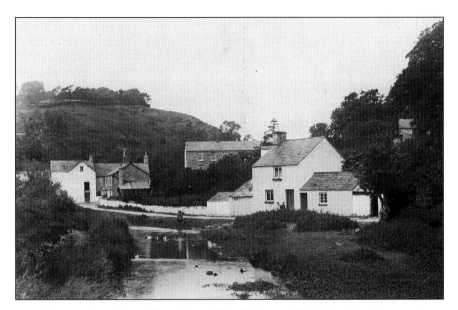

The Mill and the Old Bakehouse, about 1910

gardener, in 1740, and Morgan Rees in the 1770s. Revd John Carne wrote of his tenant, 'Morgan Rees – he owes me a year or two's rent, but is so poor I never expect or mean to be paid'. Timothy David, William Howell and John Morgan were subsequent lessees.

Various deeds locate the property as being 'on the way from the Great Bridge to the Mill, by the waterside with a good garden under the rock'. The rock face is still visible behind the house, and the photograph shows the previous course of the river Thaw, running just in front of the house.

It was still described as 'a cottage and garden', occupied by Mary Morgan, in 1840, and it was only in 1874 that first mention of the *Bakehouse* occurs, when Robert Thomas, who also farmed sixteen acres, was the occupant. In the census of 1851, this Robert Thomas, born in Pentyrch, was described as a handloom weaver employing seven workmen; in 1881 he was still described as a weaver. A literate man of some importance in the village, he had married Mary Llewellyn of *Rose Cottage* near the church; they had seven sons, one of whom, John, was the occupant in 1891, a baker and flour dealer.

He was 'Johnny the Bakehouse', still fondly remembered by some Llanblethian residents. He always wore a bowler hat when doing the baking, both of his own bread and of the bread and cakes brought in by the villagers. He or his daughter Mabel delivered the bread – two sorts of loaves, whiter than the bread from the *Mill* bakehouse – by pony and trap around the neighbouring villages. The kitchen in the house was always warm, as the bakehouse was built off the kitchen. In 1885, Johnny was mistakenly arrested for the murder of David Thomas of *Stallcourt*, only because he was out and about when the search for the murderers started. He died in 1930, a year after his wife.

The three cottages of **Greenfield Terrace** were owned in 1840 by John Williams, who also owned *Greenfield*. Though the properties are small, they have had a variety of occupants with a variety of occupations: in 1851 for example, there were a thatcher, the bailiff to Captain Boteler of Llandough Castle, and a labourer's wife; in 1861, John Elkington, a contractor from Warwickshire with his family (some of whom were here in the next two censuses). There were five families in the three cottages in 1871 - including the Nortons, later to move up the road to Broadway Hill, and Mary Thomas and family. She was a farmer's wife, and had as a lodger David Rees who had moved in from the almshouses nearby, and who had something of a reputation for filling the beds of absent husbands.

The reminiscences of Becky Jenkins, who still lives in Llanblethian, give some idea of life here in the early twentieth century:

I was born on 11th June 1909 at 3 Greenfield Terrace, Llanblethian. Mother had 13 children; two died young (George at six months, Mary at three years). The others were Ernest, Bill, Dick, John, Tom, Bert, Ada, Rachel, Peg, Dora, and of course, me. We grew up in Greenfield Terrace. The first house was occupied by Johnny John, then next-door were the Vaughans (Mrs Hilda Vaughan, large family, 10 children), then us, then the Dixons in a 1-up, 1-down cottage. When Mrs Dixon died, and Violet Dixon left, father bought that cottage to give us more room. Upstairs in No 3, the big bedroom was like a dormitory. The house had a paved front, which was kept all scrubbed right up to the gate. We grew vegetables in the garden, and at the top of the garden was the privy. This had a tin roof - my brothers used to throw stones onto the roof just to make the occupants jump!

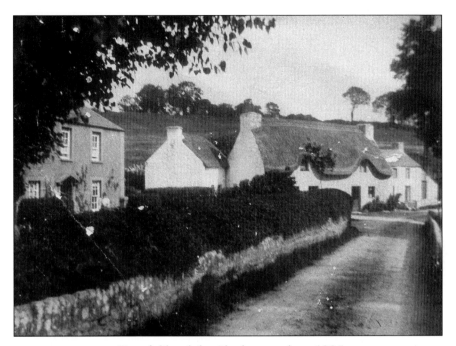

Greenfield and the Almshouses, about 1905

Just on the bridge stands **Greenfield,** a solid late-Georgian building which has been extended on the river side. This was leased (on a ninety-nine-year lease) from the Bute estate in 1834 by John Williams the mason, who also owned property in Tilla Bach (The Causeway). John Williams, not necessarily the mason, was recorded as the occupier in 1840; the John Williams who was here in 1851 was born in Bridgend according to the census, was a 'proprietor of houses', and lived here with his daughter and three grandchildren. The property is said to have been sub-let between 1840 and 1842 to Thomas Morris, 'Ten-chapel Tom', who was responsible for reviving the fortunes of *Ramoth Baptist Chapel* in Cowbridge. By 1861, the house was occupied by Dr Daniel Edwards, a London-born surgeon, and his family. He had moved before the next census, but remained in the Cowbridge area. The next known occupant was William Thomas, a bank accountant, in 1870, and then a 'Mr Loyd' in 1874 - probably William Aubrey Lloyd, also a bank official, who rose to become the manager of the

National Provincial Bank in Lampeter. Elizabeth Lloyd, his widow, was still here in 1891, with her daughter and her husband (a mariner who became Captain Thomas Morgan), who were later to live in *Cusop*.

Ann Jones, grand-daughter of the owner in 1834, lived in the house in 1910.

6: LLANBLETHIAN FARM AND GREAT HOUSE

Very little remains of **Llanblethian Farm** today - only the roadside wall of the farmhouse and some converted outbuildings, which form part of the new development of houses almost opposite *Great House*. Yet it was in that farmhouse that Hubert Thomas of Cowbridge was born, in the building earlier described by David Jones of Wallington as an 'excellent specimen of a true old Welsh farm house. First the old part of the dwelling house with one chimney; then as they grew richer a parlour, and best bedrooms added beyond that; on the other side of the kitchen came the dairy, then the barn, and lastly (in this case) the stable; all under one (thatched) roof'.

In the 1660s, this was part of the lands conveyed by the Earl of Pembroke to the Carne family of Nash and Cowbridge, and it stayed in the ownership of the Carnes until 1917.

Revd John Carne's accounts show the tenant in the 1760s to be William Jones, and in the 1770s Watkin Richard, but in 1780 Carne wrote 'Watkin being much in arrears I distrained on his goods, on which I was paid by him in full, and he this year quit the farm'. The next tenant was Evan Morgan. He had married Mary Rees, and they had five children - Rebecca, Mary (who married David Howell of Coychurch, and whose son was Dean Howell, the noted Anglican cleric), Thomas, Evan (who eventually took over the farm) and Jane, who married John Nicholas, a carpenter of Llanblethian.

Evan Morgan died in 1794, and his wife continued the lease which was taken over by Evan junior on her death in 1806. It was this younger Evan who was described by David Jones as being responsible for the ox-roast in *Great House* in honour of the Blosses; he it was who used a rope to suspend the ox over the fire, and so it was he who was blamed when the rope burned through and the carcass collapsed into the flames and ashes!

The conditions of Evan Morgan's lease of 1811 are interesting as they reflect the development of the agricultural revolution, with conditions aimed at preventing monoculture of grains, at using sainfoin or clover to restore nitrogen levels in the soil, at using lime and manure on the soil, and at using the wheat straw for the repair of the thatched roofs.

Evan gave up his tenancy in 1820, and was followed by David Davies, until the latter's death in 1843, when he was succeeded by his widow Anne. In 1851, she is described as having four daughters, one son and a servant living in the house. By 1861 the son, Ebenezer, is shown as the head of the household, employing two men and farming eighty acres. He was a man of some importance in the village, and became census enumerator in 1891.

John Jones, born in Ewenny, had taken over *Llanblethian Farm* by 1878, and had increased its area to ninety-six acres; he had two servants to look after him. He is recorded as being here at least until 1910.

Owen Williams of *Crossways* bought the property from the Carnes in about 1917, in his short-lived, initially successful but eventually ill-fated, venture into agriculture. The land was then farmed by Thomas Thomas, the father of Hubert Thomas of Cowbridge. When Owen Williams had to auction his lands in 1924, Thomas Thomas had moved into *Great House*, though he still farmed the land, and a T Brewer lived in the farmhouse.

Across the road, **Mardy** and **Ashley Cottages** were once one building, known as *The Dairy*. Long part of the *Great House* estate, it was occupied in 1840 by Thomas Jones, the father of David Jones of Wallington. It is likely that the building was sub-divided by the 1851 census, and it remained as two labourers' cottages throughout the nineteenth century. The cottages have been substantially enlarged since then.

Great House was built on land which was probably part of the property conveyed in 1668-9 by Philip, Earl of Pembroke and lord of the manor of Llanblethian, to Thomas Carne of Nash Manor and John Carne of Cowbridge. The Royal Commission on Ancient and Historic Monuments in Wales suggests that the earliest part of the house dates from about 1600, and was enlarged (to less than half its present size) in the mid-seventeenth century. The sundial on the central gable (with initials TW) is dated 1703 and probably marks the date of the building of the present house, which displays the symmetry popular in sizeable buildings of that period. It is a grade II★ listed building.

The owner in 1703 is assumed to be Thomas Wilkins, a lawyer and prothonotary (or chief clerk) on the Brecon circuit. He was the son of Revd Thomas Wilkins, the antiquary and bibliophile of St Mary Church. The initials TW and the date 1710 are carved on the kitchen fireplace;

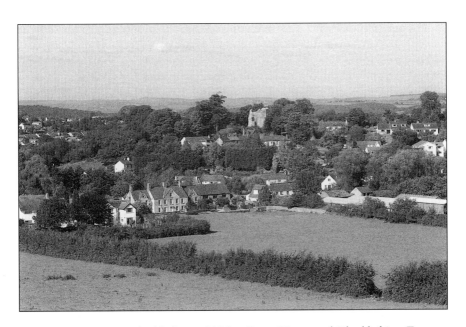

View over eastern Llanblethian, 1990s: Great House and Llanblethian Farm buildings in foreground, the Castle and St Quentin's House in background

Wilkins's name, and that of his third wife Hester, are cast on the bells of *Holy Cross Church* in Cowbridge. It was Cann Wilkins, the son of his first marriage (to Anne Cann of Compton, Gloucestershire), who sold the house in 1751 to William Bruce for £2,250.

Bruce, born in 1705 to Captain James Bruce and his wife Margaret, had been a navy agent and banker in London. After his marriage in the 1740s to Jane Lewis of Llanishen, he became interested in holding land in south Wales, and though she soon died, he purchased first the Dyffryn Aberdare estate, and then *Great House* in November 1751. He then married Mary Turberville, and they lived in *Great House* for most of the time up to 1768; he became sheriff of Glamorgan in 1756, and Commissioner of the Exchequer for much of south Wales in 1760. William Bruce died in 1768, leaving his estate to his son, Revd Thomas Bruce, rector of St Nicholas, with the proviso that Mary should have the Llanblethian property for her life.

Thomas Bruce, who was made a freeman of Cowbridge in 1770, in turn left his lands in trust for the children of his two sisters. One, Margaret, had married John Knight of Barnstaple, who helped run the Bruce family estates, and they lived in *Great House* between at least 1784 and 1797 when they moved to Bath. Their son, John Bruce Knight, born in Llanblethian in 1784, attended Cowbridge Grammar School and went on to Oxford; when he reached the age of twenty-one he changed his name to John Bruce Bruce, and later to John Bruce Pryce when he inherited the Dyffryn St Nicholas estate.

After 1797 James O'Brien was a tenant for a short time, followed by Sir Robert Blosse, an Irish baronet. David Jones of Wallington, who at one time lived at *Great House,* has a description of a memorable party held by Sir Robert: there was dancing on the lawn in front of the house (a square piece of land now part of the field across the road), and 'nearly all the County assembled there, open house being kept for a whole week or more; all the village was there to see the dancing'.

It was in 1803 when Sir Robert was the tenant that the house was sold to Major Andrew Armstrong 'late of Ireland but now of Llandough Castle'. The conveyance refers to 'a capital messuage or Mansion House together with stables, gardens and outhouses, late in the possession or occupation of James O'Brien, Esq., now or late of Sir Robert Blosse . . . and all that orchard behind the manor house, and that orchard called the little orchard lately in the possession or occupation of Mr Evan Deere and now Sir Robert Blosse . . .' as well as other crofts, barns, the adjoining cottage, then called *The Dairy*, and a close and four fields. BH Malkin in *The Scenery, Antiquities and Biography of South Wales* wrote (in 1803) 'The village of Llanblethian is remarkably rural and picturesque; while Sir Robert Lynch Blosse's little villa adds to its gaiety'.

Revd Paull and his family were, according to David Jones, the next occupants of *Great House*. They employed as a nurse Margaret Williams, the daughter of Ned the ostler at *The Bear* in Cowbridge, who had been brought up in the Darren at the western end of Cowbridge, perhaps at *Rock Cottage*. Her mother, Nancy the Darren, sold crumpets and teacakes throughout the town of Cowbridge. In looking after the children, Margaret picked up so much knowledge that she became nursery governess, and also attended the lessons provided for the eldest daughter. She eventually became governess in London to the only daughter of Lord Ponsonby, who held a high position in the affairs of state. Lady Ponsonby was unable to entertain visitors, and it was Margaret who took her place. At the Peace of 1815, it was said that, in a drawing room crowded with senior statesmen from all over Europe, she was the only person able to converse with every distinguished guest in the language of his own country.

Captain James Boorder, RN, having distinguished himself (and gained prize money) in the war against France, and being unfit for further service, purchased *Great House* in 1808. He suffered very considerably from gout and was practically immobile, and soon had to be carried about in his chair. His brother's illegitimate daughter, a beautiful actress named Mrs Careless, installed herself to look after her uncle's household, and did all she could to persuade her uncle to leave the property to her. Despite the difference in names, it seems likely that she was the 'Frances Boorder otherwise Frances Harben the reputed wife of Thomas Henry Harben Esq' named in Boorder's will and who, again according to David Jones, lived in the house for some time after Boorder's death in 1818, and then let it.

Her tenants included Captain Dawson, of the Royal Engineers, who was engaged in the trigonometrical survey of the county, and who had his men camped in half a dozen tents in the field opposite the house. Among his officers was Lieutenant Boteler who later married a Miss Casberd of Penmark; they subsequently, as Colonel and Mrs Boteler, lived at Llandough Castle. Captain Dawson married twice - first a daughter of Revd Robert Nicholl of Dimlands in Llantwit Major (but previously of *Hill House),* and secondly a daughter of John Bevan of Cowbridge.

The 1840 tithe map records Mary Ann Harbeen (probably the Frances Harben referred to above) as the owner, and William Dunn (usually spelled Donne) as occupier. The Donnes included William, his parents Mathew and Ann who had been farmers at St Donats and then Llanmihangel, and also William's older brother Thomas with his wife, and daughter by a previous marriage. The latter two seem to have played on the old people's belief in ghosts to organise mock hauntings, in an attempt to persuade Thomas to move out of quiet Llanblethian, but were exposed in a seance held in the house. By 1843 all had gone - William to Monkton farm near Monknash - and they were succeeded by the Abrahams for two years. The house was then vacant for a year until Thomas Jones, father of David Jones of Wallington, moved in from *The Dairy* next door at Christmas 1845. David Jones and his mother remained here until 1863, though his father died in 1858. It was here that David's love of Llanblethian and the Vale was nurtured.

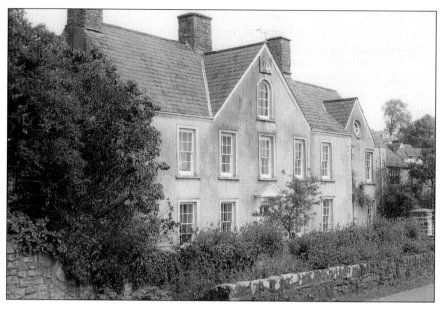

Great House

In 1862, the property was auctioned, and bought by John Bruce Pryce of Dyffryn St Nicholas, who effectively repurchased the old family home. David Jones's comments were: 'When old Bruce Pryce called on me in 1862, and went over the house even into the garrets, he said he wondered how Sir Robert Blosse's magnificent flunkeys - and he kept several such - had managed to put up with such miserable sleeping quarters as they must have had in those unceiled garrets'. Bruce Pryce died in 1872, and the house and lands were auctioned in 1877 and sold to John Truman Jenkins of St y Nill. Jenkins died in the following year, and the property was again put up for auction in 1879. It was bought by William Morgan, farmer and butcher, for £2,500. William was the son of Robert Morgan, the butcher, of *Causeway Cottages*, and in the 1871 census was farming at *Porth y Green*. (At that time, *Great House* was occupied by John Morgan, a forty-seven-year-old farmer born in Llanblethian, and his family).

The 1881 census shows that William, a farmer of forty acres and a butcher, lived here with his wife Rebecca, born in Llandow, and their nine children who varied in age from eighteen years to nine months. In 1890, it was yet again auctioned, and William moved to 50 High Street in Cowbridge. The purchaser was Robert Williams, a retired innkeeper from Llanbethery, who obtained a mortgage from Revd Thomas Edmondes of *Old Hall*. Williams could not keep up with the repayments, so Edmondes foreclosed on the mortgage, and sold *Great House* to William Hancock and Co. During their period of ownership, 1893 to 1911, the occupant was the chairman of Hancocks, Joseph Gaskell.

The following years saw more changes of ownership. The property went firstly to William Henry Mathias of Tynycymmer Hall, Porth, from 1911 to 1920, and then to Owen Williams of *Crossways*, the shipping magnate, from 1920 to 1924. *Great House*, at the time divided into two, and occupied by Thomas Thomas and George Morris, was then auctioned in a desperate attempt to raise some funds to offset the decline in Williams's fortune; he had bought it for £4,000 but only obtained £2,000 in the auction. Mrs Mary Morgan of 68 Eastgate, Cowbridge, wife of Robert Morgan the butcher, purchased *Great House*. Once again the house reverted to the family of a previous owner, as Robert was the son of William Morgan who had owned the house and lived here from 1879 to 1890. Robert was living in *Great House* by 1926. The adjacent barn (now a separate dwelling) was used as the slaughterhouse: the quality of Robert Morgan's black puddings was celebrated in the area.

In 1943, the house was purchased by Mrs Carne and Mrs Prichard. Mrs Prichard's son had married Rosemary Christie, the daughter of Agatha Christie; their son is Matthew Prichard of Pwllywrach, Colwinston.

7: ST QUENTIN'S HILL TO BROADWAY FARM

Just up the hill from the *Mill* stands **The Firs**, a substantial building of some age. There appear to be few early documents relating to the property. We are sure, however, that in 1840 it was owned and lived in by Mary Thomas. She continued to own the house, but in 1851 (and also in 1861) it was occupied by Thomas Prichard, a gardener from west Wales, his wife and his son, also a gardener. James Braddick from Stockland in Devon (one of a number of people from Stockland who settled in Llanblethian in the nineteenth century) was in *The Firs* by 1871, with his second wife Eliza, née James. They had moved from a cottage on Factory Road. Braddick was initially a servant in *Llanblethian House*, then was described as a coachman, but after the move to *The Firs* he became a gardener, and

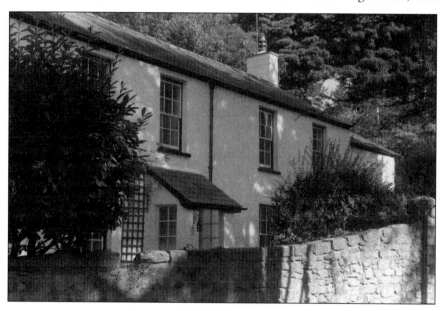

The Firs

cultivated his large garden on the opposite side of the road. (It is today the garden of *St Quentin's Cottage*). He did well enough to win prizes at the Cottagers' vegetable shows in the village.

When Mrs Braddick died in 1909 (James had died earlier) the house was conveyed to Thomas Butler of Prisk, and the garden sold off to George Williams of *Brooklyn* in Piccadilly. The house then had a rapid succession of tenants, among them Mrs S Nicholl, the Misses Llewellyn, Mrs Llewellyn, and Revd James McLauchlan, the Wesleyan minister, in 1926.

The cottages which existed on the site of **St Quentin's Terrace** were depicted in the Bucks engraving of *Llanblethian Castle* in the 1740s. In 1840, they were owned by William Royds, who also owned *St Quentin's House* opposite; they were essentially labourers' cottages. A rebuild at the end of the century, by WA James the Cowbridge builder, created the terrace, with a larger *The Cairns* (recently sympathetically extended) at the east end.

St Quentin's House is situated on the corner of Castle Hill and St Quentin's Hill. Its rather drab façade to the street is almost devoid of windows. However, hidden behind high stone walls is the south face, overlooking a series of terraces in the garden, and enjoying views over lower Llanblethian and the hillside beyond. Built with stone taken from the castle, the house would appear to have started as a much smaller building than that of today, being gradually added to over the years. A surviving seventeenth-century frieze and early Georgian window frames are evidence of some of the construction stages. There is a vaulted cellar with two entrances in the form of circular staircases.

The house has had a rich history, illustrated by its various owners and residents. The earliest record of occupants is of 1820, when Captain Hugh Eccles, a one-armed survivor of the Peninsular war, lived here with his young family. Two of his children were baptised in Llanblethian church. After moving to Bath, the family emigrated to Canada in 1835, where sons Henry and William became prominent lawyers.

In 1825, Captain William Royds, one of the Rochdale families who were to play a great part in the life of Llanblethian in the nineteenth century, was installed in the house. When he married Georgiana Peel (niece of Sir Robert Peel, the Prime Minister, whose name gave early policemen the nickname 'Peelers') at Clifton that same year, he was

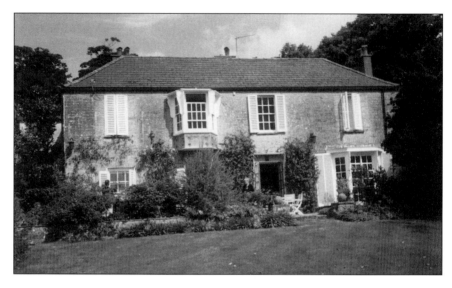

St Quentin's House

described as 'Captain Royds of Llanblethian', but though he continued to own the house he did not live here long. By 1828 it had been let to one of the Peel family, and then became the home of Revd Rees Howell, vicar of Llancarfan and curate of Cowbridge. When he died in 1830, his baby son was only a few days old and was christened over his father's coffin. His widow, Harriet Anne, was the daughter of William Williams, the headmaster of Cowbridge Grammar School. In 1836, a letter stated 'Rumour is very busy marrying Mrs Howell to the clergyman of this parish – she is looking very well and gay', and indeed in 1838 Harriet Howell married Revd Thomas Edmondes, vicar of Llanblethian and Cowbridge, and three sons were born to the couple. After several years in *St Quentin's House*, the family moved to live in *Old Hall* in Cowbridge, following the death of the father of Thomas (Major Thomas Edmondes).

Revd Thomas Edmondes went on to become the 'uncrowned king' of Cowbridge. He remained vicar until 1884, and was an alderman and a freeman, as were two of his sons and his step-son. Of his three sons born while he lived in *St Quentin's House*, Charles became Archdeacon of St David's and principal of Lampeter College, Frederic became Archdeacon of Llandaff, but refused the position of bishop, and Francis entered the army.

In 1851, John Samuel, an eighty-year-old landowner born in Penmark, was the tenant here, living with his niece and a servant. The death of Lt-Colonel William Royds in 1858 (who left the property in the hands of trustees) saw a change of occupants. His son, Frederick Charles Alton Royds (born in Clemenstone, Llandow in 1827) then lived in *St Quentin's House* with his wife Frances, but in January 1863, when hunting with the Duke of Beaufort's hunt at Tetbury in Gloucestershire, he was thrown from his horse and killed. He had been Lieutenant of the Cowbridge Rifle Corps where, according to the *Central Glamorgan Gazette*:

the entire command of the corps devolved upon him. So well did he perform those duties that he was universally loved by the men under his command. His urbanity of temper and general bearing towards his men so won their admiration and esteem that it was unanimously determined by them, according to time-honoured custom, to proceed to church to pay the last tribute of respect to their departed officer, Accordingly on Sunday last, the members of the Corps met at the Town Hall, each man wearing a badge of black crepe around his left arm, and preceded by their brass band marched to the parish church, where a very affecting and impressive sermon was preached by the Revd Thomas Edmondes, the respected vicar . . . The same sad solemn spectacle was re-enacted in the afternoon, at Llanblethian church, where a very appropriate sermon was preached by the Revd John Evans, who drew a beautiful picture of the deceased in his capacity of soldier, magistrate, Christian and gentleman.

By the mid-1860s Titus Lewis had moved to the house with his family of three sons and three daughters. Previously, he had owned a draper's shop in Carmarthen, but the business had failed and he became a commercial traveller. However, he is better remembered as a Welsh poet. He translated a great number of English hymns into Welsh, and several of his poems were published, including *The Soldier's Wife, a Tale of Inkerman*. The National Library of Wales at Aberystwyth holds a large collection of his work. By the 1871 census, one of the Lewis boys was an Oxford graduate, and the other an undergraduate at Lampeter. Titus died in 1887, but his widow Catherine stayed on in the house until she was succeeded by Richard Mathias and his wife, three children and two servants. Mathias was in charge of the building of the Cowbridge railway extension to Aberthaw.

In 1894, Harold Bird was living in *St Quentin's House;* he was the district surveyor for Cowbridge and took over the ironmonger's shop, which eventually became a noted lawn-mower business, in the town. A number of annual tenants followed Bird. In 1918, Revd William Franklen Evans retired after twenty-eight years as a loved and respected headmaster of Cowbridge Grammar School, and came to live in the house, a somewhat exhausted man after years of struggle with the authorities regarding the well-being of the school. He died in 1929.

Annie and Stanley Philpot were the next occupants. He was a landscape architect and was probably responsible for laying out the garden in its present form. Both died in 1943; theirs is the tallest tombstone in Llanblethian churchyard.

Following the death of her husband, Blanche Homfray came from Penllyn Castle to live in *St Quentin's House* with her Yorkshire terrier called 'John Peel'. Her son-in-law was JC Clay, the Glamorgan and England cricketer. When she died in 1947, the house was purchased by Francis and Ronald Walters, two brothers who owned several shoe shops in the area, who subsequently sold it to Sir David and Lady Joan Llewellyn. He was MP for Cardiff North, and Under-Secretary for Welsh Affairs at the Home Office. For twenty-seven years he also wrote a weekly horse racing column in *Sporting Life* under the pseudonym of 'Jack Logan'. Sir David, a Conservative MP, sided with a Labour MP, George Thomas (later to become Speaker of the House of Commons) in objecting to certain actions of Welsh nationalists, with the consequence that the inhabitants of Llanblethian woke one morning to find the garden walls of *St Quentin's House* daubed with Welsh graffiti. Lady Joan is the niece of Blanche Homfray. Between 1942 and 1946, she was in charge of the War Cabinet Cipher Office, and accompanied Winston Churchill to conferences in Marrakesh and Quebec.

It was during the Llewellyn's time in the house that a number of famous people came to stay - the Bishop of Exeter, the authors Naomi Jacob and Pamela Frankau, JPL Thomas (Lord Cilcennin), Field Marshal Earl Alexander of Tunis, the actor Boris Karloff, the Duke of Bedford and Raine Lewisham (Countess of Dartmouth, Countess Spencer etc). Another famous guest was Mrs Pandit, sister of Jawaharlal Nehru, Prime Minister of India. She stayed in the house in 1957 while her attendant, Gurbachan Singh, slept across the lane in *Thimble Cottage*, which the Llewellyns had built for their gardener. Singh was responsible for Mrs Pandit's safety: it was the beginning of a tradition whereby Sikhs were chosen for this protective role. Sadly, it was Sikh members of her bodyguard who assassinated her niece, Indira Gandhi.

Dominating this part of Llanblethian, **St Quentin's Castle** stands at the western edge of a limestone ridge, with steep slopes running down to the river Thaw. It is the eastern end which would have been most vulnerable to attack, and so here stands the fine gatehouse of the castle, erected around 1300 by the de Clares. The *inquisition post mortem* on the death of Gilbert de Clare in 1314 refers to the castle 'begun by the earl'.

There was however a much earlier building, which gives the castle its present name. Behind the gatehouse are the remains of the stone keep, built by the St Quentins, lords of Llanblethian in the early twelfth century. One of Colonel Taynton's watercolours, mentioned earlier, showed the keep standing nearly as high as the gatehouse in 1852. The St Quentin property in Glamorgan was taken over by Richard Siward in 1233; Siward's lands were seized by Earl Richard de Clare in 1245.

The de Clare castle was never completed, but recent work by CADW, who now manage the site on behalf of the National Assembly for Wales (it was taken into care in 1994 after a sustained campaign in the neighbourhood), shows clearly what the castle would have looked like. An impressive curtain wall, offering protection on the north, west and south, has been cleared of debris; it enclosed a sizeable area. The gatehouse, which has now been stabilised and sympathetically conserved, was probably complete by 1314. It is regarded as one of the best examples of its kind in Wales, with high quality masonry. Builders' marks are still clearly to be seen on the quoins of the building.

CADW have used local lias limestone, now slightly darker than the original stone (but it will soon weather) to renew the stonework where this was dictated for safety reasons; recessed joints make clear what is old and what is new.

There are two towers in the gatehouse, and the entrance passage was defended by two portcullises and a murder slot. In the base of the southern tower, a guard chamber was converted into a prison; the first floor was probably a military guardroom, while the missing second floor is likely to have contained residential quarters. Away from the gatehouse, the north-east tower, now cut into by the modern entrance to the castle grounds, was once of two storeys, and also housed residential accommodation.

The gatehouse was used as a prison in the sixteenth century, and thereafter it served as a house, a public house (as quoted by David Jones), and farm buildings. In the nineteenth century the grounds were the scene of Llanblethian's flower and vegetable shows. A report in the *Glamorgan Gazette* in 1866 stated:

The turfed terraces of the castle were not only found pretty but useful in the display of flowers, as also the verdure-clad shelving which enriches the open space. From the castle keep the royal standard

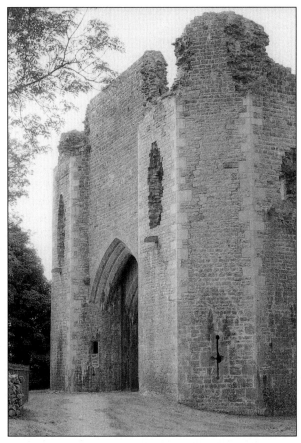

St Quentin's Castle, 2001

fluttered, and many coloured flags and pennants floated gaily in the breeze. At intervals the band of the 18th Glamorgan Volunteers, under the leadership of Sergeant Williams, played selections of music. In prominent positions, the following mottoes were disposed – 'Success to the Cottage Garden Exhibition', 'The hand of the diligent maketh rich'.

The castle was also of significance as a major 'quarry' for building stone in this part of the village. **Castle Cottage** is claimed to be constructed entirely of stone from the castle. It had been bought, in ruins, by Jane Vallance, a wealthy Cowbridge widow, from William Bruce in 1752, and later transferred to Elizabeth Wilkins, Jane's mother. By 1840 it had been rebuilt and was part of the landholdings of Revd Edward Morgan of *The Verlands*, and was the home of David Williams, a labourer born in Llanblethian, and his family. Unrecorded in 1861, the house was occupied in 1871 and for at least ten years thereafter by John Eddolls, a miller from Penmark and his family. Later occupants were William Robert, also a labourer, Mr Jones, a gardener in *The Verlands*, and Isaac Thomas, carpenter and builder, who had moved from *Leys Cottage* in Factory Road.

Just below the cottage, the old manorial pound (used for keeping stray animals) now houses an electricity sub-station. Finds of green-glazed medieval pottery in the field behind *Castle Cottage* suggest that there was a settlement here in the early Middle Ages, grouped around what would have been the main access road leading directly to the gatehouse of the castle. It has been suggested that very much later, in the Victorian era, the Bute estate grew grapes for wine in greenhouses behind the tall roadside wall.

In the eighteenth century, **Porth y Green** was the property of the Caercady estate, though early tax assessments do not mention the existence of a house upon the spot. David Jones of Wallington, however, writes of the house being here in the early nineteenth century. He claimed it had been built of stone from the castle, and that there had been a sizeable ruin, on both sides of the road, before the house was built. Two sculptured heads incorporated within the garden doorway are also reputed to originate from the castle. The present appearance of the house indicates a late-Victorian modernisation.

The John Jenkins who lived at *Porth y Green* in the early years of the nineteenth century had been a haberdasher and draper in Cowbridge, and

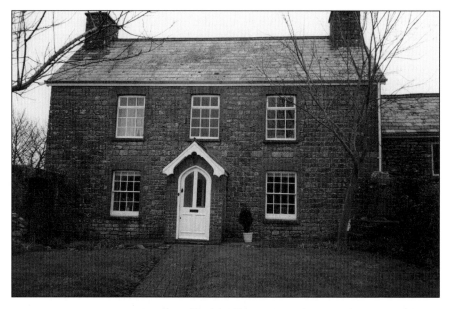

Porth y Green

he stored his remaining stock in one of the rooms of *St Quentin's Castle*. This stock included gilt shoe buckles, which he would occasionally give out as presents to the local children - leading to rumours of buried treasure in the castle. William Evans and his wife Nancy lived in the house with Mr Jenkins, and continued here after his death.

By 1851, William Davies, a retired maltster, born in Mynyddislwyn, with his Cowbridge-born wife Mary, three children and a grand-daughter, lived in *Porth y Green*. The older daughter, Eliza, was a school teacher and had been born in Cowbridge, the younger Joseph and Ellen in Mynyddislwyn.

They were replaced by the following census by a widow, Eliza Lloyd, born in Reading, and her three daughters, all of whom had been born in Gloucester. Mrs Lloyd died in 1870, and William Morgan then occupied the house. He was a butcher, the son of Richard Morgan of the Causeway in Llanblethian, and also farmed the six fields associated with the house. In the 1871 census, he and his wife Rebecca, born in Llandow, are shown as having four children. The Morgans - who were to be butchers in Cowbridge for most of the twentieth century - moved to *Great House* between 1877 (when the Caercady estate sold the house and land) and 1881.

Bennett Edwards, a thirty-two-year-old farmer of twenty acres, born in Cowbridge, had moved into the house from Factory Road by 1881; Edwardses were to live in *Porth y Green* for the next eighty years. Bennett stayed a farmer, but Evan, the oldest son, became a butcher, and 'Edwards the butchers' was a thriving shop in Eastgate, Cowbridge until the 1970s.

While **Broadway Farm** is obviously one of the few old properties to be seen on Broadway today, its origins are somewhat hazy. The fields in which the house was built were known as 'Cecil Woodward's lands' in the eighteenth century; they were owned by William Bruce of *Great House* and leased to a variety of tenants. Rees Adam of *Stallcourt* farmed the land in 1799, but at that time it was leased to Henry Edmund, initially described as a yeoman, but later a cooper. Edmund acquired the land and left it in his will to his children.

One of his children, Mary, had married Evan Hopkin in 1824, and in 1840 Evan Hopkin is recorded as the occupier of the house and garden - so far, this is the first record that we have of a building on the site.

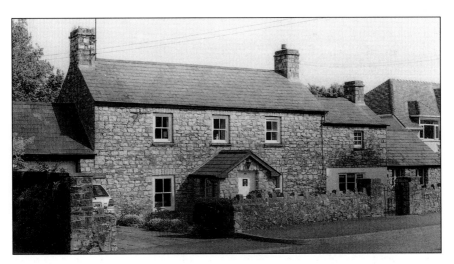

Broadway Farm

There is remarkable stability of occupation here, as Evan (born about 1798 in Llysworney) is shown as living in the farmhouse from 1840 to at least 1881. He farmed at most fifteen acres. In 1851, he and his wife had a servant, Mary Evans, and two nieces, probably twins - Mary and Rebecca Griffiths born in Llanharan - living with them. Mary Hopkin died in 1857, and in 1861 Mary Williams, a widow born in Colwinston, was his housekeeper, and remained so until his death.

The farm was sold in 1881, with Evan Hopkin as sitting tenant, to Revd D Watkin Williams of Pontypridd, and became part of a larger estate, including *The Verlands*. Thomas Whitney farmed here in 1890, and the 1891 census records the house in two parts - one occupied by Thomas Whitney's widow Mary Ann, who described herself as a dairy farmer, aged sixty-seven, born in Llanblethian, and the other part by her children - two daughters and a son, James, his wife and their two children.

By 1910 George Cox and his son David were living here. George died in 1930, at the age of eighty-one, but his son David continued running the farm.

Many still think of the building as 'Meredith's shop', a favourite calling point for children in more recent years on their way to and from school in Broadway. It is now a private residence.

8: BROADWAY HILL

Cusop obviously had a late-Victorian make-over, but there were two cottages on this site in 1824, part of the Bute estate. The tenant of both was James Bird, ironmonger of Cowbridge, and he sub-let them.

In 1851, George Sandland, a gamekeeper from Warwickshire and his wife Ann, who later moved to *Hillside*, lived in the top cottage, now part of *Cusop*. They had as a lodger Edwin Usher, a twenty-two-year-old huntsman born in Weston-super-Mare, and who was later to move down to *Bridge Farm*. Among the large number of subsequent tenants were James Chard, a thirty-six-year-old plumber and gasfitter, born in Bristol, who lived here in 1881 with his wife and six children (those of four years and under having been born in Llanblethian), and in 1891 James Eddolls, aged

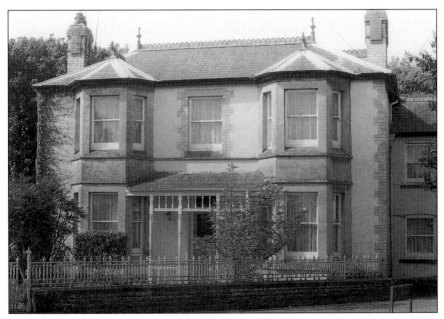

Cusop

sixty-five, a labourer from Penmark, with his wife, two sons and one grandson. (James's brother John had earlier been in *Castle Cottage*).

By 1895, the house had been purchased from Nathaniel Bird by William Rees, a Rhondda-based brewer who added the front part of the property, lived here, and named it *Rhondda Villa*. The name '*Cusop*' came later, when the Morgans lived here. Cyril Morgan's chickens, roaming around Windmill Lane and the adjoining land, are still remembered with a smile.

Next door, in **Mere Cottage**, there was again a rapid succession of tenants: John Rice from Swansea in 1840, the forty-five-year-old Alice Williams, born in Welsh St Donats, with her three children in 1851, and within a year a Mrs George. Later there was some greater continuity of occupancy. Thomas Deere, born in Porthkerry in 1831, lived here at least from 1881 to 1895, with his wife Mary Ann (née George), her mother, who was described as a pauper, their daughter, and two boarders. William Lewis and his wife were to follow them for the first half of the twentieth century.

Just down the hill, **Broadway House** was owned in 1840 by James Bird, who had gained a considerable interest in property in this part of Broadway. Then tenanted by Edward Griffiths, by 1851 the house was occupied by Martha Jones, a widow and farmer of fifteen acres, with her four children. Martha had been born in Coity, but all her children were born in Ewenny - which helps us to trace them through subsequent census listings. John, Peggy (Margaret) and Anne Jones were here in 1859; John farmed twenty acres in 1861, and in 1871 William, also born in Ewenny, and so who perhaps was another brother, farmed thirty-nine acres. William Jones stayed in the house until his death in 1905, when William Norton, who had a carpentry business in Cowbridge, moved in from the cottage lower down the hill. With William and his wife came their young niece Eveline Hopkin, who became a great character with a fund of information about old Llanblethian.

She has told us about whitewashing the cistern under the back yard, which was the main source of water, blackleading the grate, baking jam turnovers in a Dutch oven in front of the fire, killing two pigs a year and salting the bacon and ham, making cheese and butter - because they also farmed the land across the road.

The pair of cottages further down the hill, now *Ar y Bryn* and *Lake Hill Cottage*, are recorded in the Dunraven estate map of 1779 as 'a cottage on the waste, occupied by Evan William'; in 1811 the property was conveyed by John Wyndham of Dunraven to John Thomas, a wine merchant of Bristol. In 1840, James Bird was recorded as the owner, and Robert Bowen - a farm labourer from Pyle - occupied the house with his wife and daughter; they were also here in 1852. Between that date and 1881, the house was probably rebuilt as two cottages. In 1891 they were occupied by two William Nortons - the thirty-four-year-old carpenter, born in Llanblethian, and his wife Susannah, who were to move next door to *Broadway House* - and his father, a fifty-nine-year-old tailor, born in Cowbridge, with his wife Ann and grandson, also named William.

In 1895, the carpenter Norton was still in occupation, but the other Norton had been replaced by Edward Evans who is recorded as owner and occupier, though it was really held on a long lease, and in 1913 the cottages were sold by the Dunraven estate. Subsequently, but only for a short period, they were part of the estate of Owen Williams of *Crossways*.

Further down the hill, **Bridge House** has late-medieval origins; on the side facing the road a projection (an outshut) contains a stone staircase. The house is marked on the Dunraven estate map of 1767, though not as part of the estate. In the tithe map of 1840, John Williams was the tenant of the house and two adjoining fields, which were owned by James Taylor of *Cowbridge Town Mill*. In 1851, Thomas Butler, a coal carrier and farmer of three acres, was the occupant, and he was followed by 1861 (and at least up until 1874) by Thomas Whitney, who was later to move to *Broadway Farm*.

By 1881, Edwin Usher (who in 1851 was a lodger in *Cusop*) lived in the house, and farmed twenty-five acres. He was still here in 1910 even though the valuation of that date considered the house a ruin. When he died in 1921, aged ninety-four, he had been churchwarden at Llanblethian church for twenty-nine years. The farm temporarily became part of Owen Williams's *Crossways* estate, but was sold in 1924. It is now a private house.

On the other side of the road from *Bridge Farm* were four thatched cottages; the site of the last is now a small council-maintained garden. The two middle cottages were **Almshouses**, labelled as 'Poor House' on the 1779 Dunraven estate map. A plaque in the centre of the building had the date 1727 on it with the inscription 'Remember ye Poor'. Thatching the

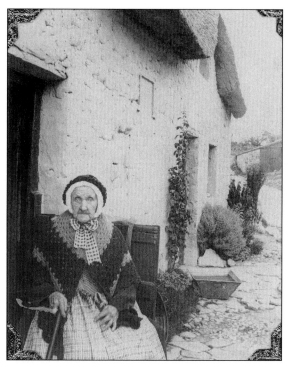

'Bopa' Lewis outside the Almshouses, 1899

cottages in 1868 cost the Llanblethian churchwardens £3. 2s. 4½d. Among the noteworthy residents were Catherine Rees in 1851, then a seventy-three-year-old pauper farm labourer's widow, who according to David Jones, had 'gullied' on the parish for years. Jones also claimed that her son had fathered David Roberts, the murderer of Thomas of *Stallcourt*. In 1871, seventy-two-year-old Jane (or Bopa) Lewis moved into one of the almshouses; she died here at the age of 102.

Early in the twentieth century, the two almshouses were occupied by Mrs Haig and Mr Groom. Becky Jenkins of Llanblethian remembers them thus:

Ma Haig was an old Irish woman, who used to laugh and joke with children who were playing on the bridge. When she went in, boys would play tricks on her - tying a button onto cotton and using it to tap on the window - because they knew she'd rush out swearing. Next door was Mr Groom, a dear old man who looked like a tramp. He used to catch rabbits and skin them, and he slept on the floor. We used to love looking in through the windows to see him lying on his pile of sacks. Mother used to make cake for him, which we children would take round.

Miss Eveline Hopkin of *Broadway House* remembered Mrs Haig as 'a dear lady wearing a man's cap, and a Welsh woollen shawl put three-cornered over her shoulders, with a clean canvas apron - and her face shone. She had a beautiful complexion. She loved her bottle of stout on a Saturday night. She did our washing for thirty years'.

Another reminiscence - of Mrs Tonkin of Stalling Down - was of Mrs Haig driving her donkey cart to the *Railway Inn* in Cowbridge, and later emerging from the inn to find that some lads had put the donkey back-to-front in the cart shafts.

The one-up, one-down cottage now replaced by a garden was for much of the mid-twentieth century known as *Aunt Em's*, as it was occupied by Emily Royall. Before her, Ted and May Surrey lived here, with their crippled daughter Mary Jane, who occupied her time by sewing. The Vaughan children from Greenfield Terrace used to annoy old Ted, by climbing on the roof and putting sacking over the chimney to make smoke billow out into the downstairs room. However, Ted had a vicious cockerel to make sure honours were even. He was known as 'a character'; he is pictured on the back cover of this book.

9 : TO THE WEST OF THE VILLAGE

Of the small cluster of buildings at the *Cross Inn* crossroads, only the inn itself and *Pentwyn* are of any antiquity, and their history has proved difficult to trace back before the 1840 tithe apportionment.

In 1840, **Cross Inn** was owned and occupied by John Marchant, who also farmed a neighbouring field. Evan Morgan is named as the victualler

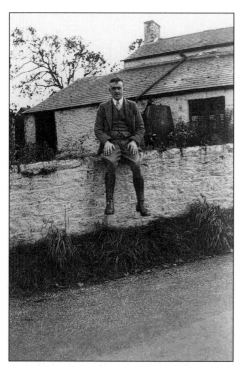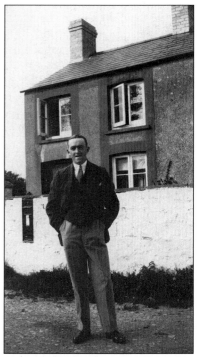

Cross Inn, late 1930s, with Wyndham James

from 1851 to 1853, and Morgan Joseph, from Monknash, was here in the early 1870s. By 1879 Joseph (who in 1875 was named as an innkeeper and limeburner) had moved to *Limefield House* on the lane to *Crossways*, and William James from Llysworney had moved in as innkeeper, with his second wife and eight children. The James family continued to run the inn until the late 1950s. Kate, William's daughter, was the licensee from 1908 to 1916, while Martha, William's daughter-in-law, ran the business from about 1920 to 1951, and then her second husband, Bill Powell, took over until his death as a result of injuries received in a vicious attack in the inn.

The public house was owned in the mid- and late nineteenth century by William Thomas (a nephew of William Thomas of *Hill House*) who farmed first in Marcross and then the 1,100-acre Cog Farm in Sully, where he proved to be an expert cattle breeder - and often won prizes at the annual Cowbridge agricultural show. Ownership later changed to Lewis Jenkins of Cowbridge.

The core of the inn has not changed a great deal over the past fifty years. The present car park used to be a vegetable garden, surrounded by a high white-washed wall in which was set a postbox. Inside the public house, the beer was served from barrels set up on trestles in what is now the dining room.

The nearby **Pentwyn** was owned in 1840 by Revd Evan Jones, the vicar of Colwinston, who had considerable land and property investments in the Vale of Glamorgan. The occupants throughout the nineteenth century were Hopkinses: in 1840, John Hopkins, a labourer from Llysworney, and his wife Margaret. They were still here in 1851, but then their son David, a mason, was living in a cottage next to the *Cross Inn*, with his wife Jane, and son John; these had moved into *Pentwyn* by 1861. By the next census, John had married, and had a son, Evan Thomas. Jane Hopkins died in 1872, and David in 1876; John stayed on in *Pentwyn*, and was described in 1881 as a stone cutter, and in 1891 as a builder. He and his son ET Hopkins carried on a business as monumental masons, with their yard near the river in Cowbridge. ET Hopkins moved to *The Armoury* in Cowbridge, and later *The Shield*, in the early years of the twentieth century.

Mary Jane Hopkins, John's daughter, married WE Jones, a mining engineer who, on his return from South Africa, opened first a cycle shop at 50 High Street in Cowbridge, and then the *West End Garage* in 56 High

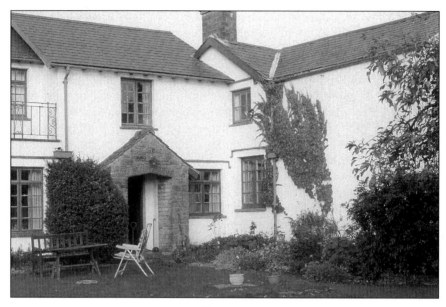

Pentwyn

Street. They lived in *Pentwyn*, initially with John Hopkins until his death in 1921. Mary's death in 1956 ended the long Hopkins connection with the house.

Settlement on the lands of **Breach Farm** occurred as early as the Bronze Age. The road from *Cross Inn* to Nash cut through a number of tumuli or burial mounds; excavation of one of these round barrows in 1937 showed that the turf and clay mound enclosed a circular stone wall. This in turn surrounded a central cremation pit containing bronze implements and flint arrowheads. The finds are now in the National Museum at Cardiff.

The farmhouse, a grade II listed building, dates from the mid-seventeenth century, and has gabled dormer windows. Its nicely carved doorway is covered with a porch, to the left of which a three-light window, with stone mullions and hoodmoulds, gives light onto the hall or main ground-floor room of the house. Internally, stone stairs, beams and a clay bake-oven add to the charm of the building.

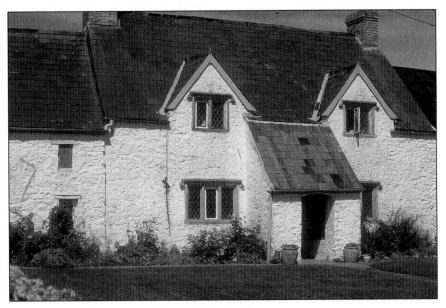

Breach Farm

The first reference that we find to *Breach* is in the will of Robert Savours 'of *Breach*', which was proved in 1711; the house stayed in the possession of the Savours family until well into the nineteenth century. Throughout most of the eighteenth century, the occupants were the Williams family, originally of Llysworney. John Williams (1700-1785), son of Henry Williams of Llanishen, gentleman, lived here in 1721; he had married Mary Jenkins of Stembridge. As well as his lease of *Breach*, he also leased land in Llysworney, St Mary Church and Newton Nottage and, as the Carne fortunes declined, he acquired more and more land in Llysworney. He was friendly with Howell Harris, one of the fathers of Welsh Methodism, and also helped to arrange for one of the circulating schools of Gruffydd Jones to be held in Llanblethian (1738-39) and Llysworney (1757-58). Of their children, Elizabeth married Robert Taynton of Cowbridge, a naval lieutenant, while Thomas, a graduate of Jesus College, Oxford, became headmaster of Cowbridge Grammar School on the resignation of Daniel Durel in 1763, and held that post until his death in 1783.

It would seem that after the death of John Williams, the subsequent occupants were William Hopkin for the rest of the eighteenth century, and then Edward Lewis between 1804 and 1821.

By 1840, it was being farmed as part of Hugh Entwisle's *Marlborough* estate, with no named occupant of the house. In the 1851 census, however, the resident farmer (of seventy-seven acres) was Daniel Thomas of St Brides. In 1861 Richard Howell of Cadoxton, Neath, was here with his wife, two sons and two servants. Richard and his wife died in 1864 and 1865 respectively, but the farm was taken over by the sons, with Rees Howell named as head of household in 1871. William Jenkins and David Evans were tenants for a short time, before Morgan Griffiths, from Maesteg, came in about 1880. Henry Jones, born in Llysworney, and his wife Elizabeth from Llanblethian, had been installed by 1884; in the 1891 census they are shown as having one domestic servant and two farm servants. The Joneses were still farming *Breach* in 1906, though by 1913 Henry Jones had retired to *Duffryn* in The Causeway, and George Rees had taken over, and then for a short time it was leased by Owen Williams as part of his large *Crossways* estate.

The last tenuous link with the Savours family as owners was severed with the death of Anne Howe of St Mary Church in 1886 (a Joseph How had married Mary Savours about 1800) when it passed to the Morgans of Woolcombe in Somerset. In 1930 *Breach Farm* was purchased by Glamorgan County Council as one of their smallholdings, and only reverted to private ownership towards the end of the twentieth century.

Marlborough Grange is a large and solid apparently Georgian building, standing just south of the Llantwit Major road beyond *Cross Inn*. The western part of the house, rubble-built and covered with stucco, and slate-hung on the side of the prevailing winds, is probably the original farmhouse, with three storeys of relatively low-ceilinged rooms, and is likely to be of eighteenth-century origin. The eastern part is of more substantial stonework, again stuccoed, and of only two storeys, with rooms of considerable height. Many of the farm buildings are of solid late-Victorian dressed stonework.

It is claimed that a Jenkins family lived in *Marlborough* in about 1800; they went to London, and Jenkins became the builder responsible for the repairs to Windsor Castle under Jeffry Wyatt the architect, in the time of George IV. William Howell was recorded as owner and occupier from

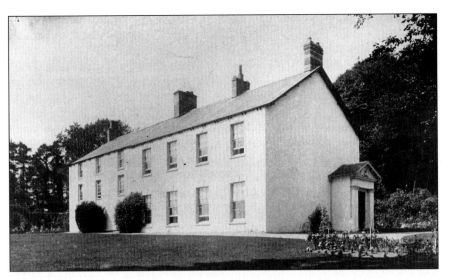

Marlborough Grange

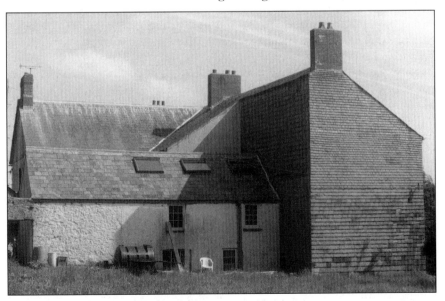

Marlborough Grange from the west

1804, and he was succeeded in 1838 by Hugh Entwisle, a retired naval commander, one of the four members of that Rochdale family who had moved into the Vale by the 1820s.

Hugh had lived in Clemenstone and in *Llanblethian Cottage* before taking over *Marlborough Grange*. By 1840, his brother Robert and sister Margaret were farming *Crossways*, the farm to the north. *Marlborough Grange* ran to 192 acres, and Hugh Entwisle rented more land nearby. In 1851, he employed ten men and a boy. On his death in 1867 it was stated that he was probably the most successful farmer in the Vale of Glamorgan, and that his crops and stock were the admiration of all who saw them. As a JP and a churchwarden, he played a full part in the life of the county and the village; as a huntsman he was well-known. At Drymma, his earlier home near Neath, he had imported a pack of hounds from Lancashire; before he moved to Llanblethian he had enquired of the Earl of Dunraven for permission to hunt west of the Ogmore river. His obituary records him as Master of the Cowbridge Harriers, and writes of 'his pleasant bearing when he followed them – his hunting horn fastened to the pommel of his saddle – welcomed to their lands by every farmer in the Vale of Glamorgan'.

His wife, Mary Anne, one of the Royds family of Rochdale who inter-married with the Entwisles and who also settled in Llanblethian, lived on in the house with her sister Frances until her death in 1878.

Recorded occupants after the Entwisles include Richard Knight Prichard, a magistrate (1884-90), Frank James, (1891-96) and William and Mary John (1908-26). The Johns used to keep a coach drawn by four black horses, in rivalry with the coach and four white horses of *Crossways*.

Ownership however became a little complicated, with the Entwisle trustees apparently agreeing to sell to William Morgan, son of Revd Jonathan Morgan, rector of Hedley in Surrey, and originally of Llysworney. William's memorial stone in Llysworney churchyard records him as vice-president of Magdalen College, Oxford. There are no records of the sale being completed, and it needed a solicitor's declaration to make it possible for the land to be sold in 1930 to Glamorgan County Council, who at that time were creating 'county smallholdings' to give people an opportunity to farm land as tenants.

The smallholdings were run successfully for about sixty years. They were sold off by the local authority in the late twentieth century, and

Marlborough land was split up between the *Grange* and a new farm based on *Marlborough Lodge*. The *Grange* building is divided, with one family occupying the eastern part, and another in the western part of the house.

Crossways, situated on the back road leading from *Cross Inn* to Llysworney, has the appearance of a mansion built about 1900, with some additions and changes since that date, but the core of the house is much older. Parts date back to Tudor times, and the first document naming *Crossways* is of 1700. Then it was owned by Edward Deere, one of the family of landowners of the Vale of Glamorgan whose interests included *Llanquian* (near Stalling Down) and Llantwit Major as well as *Crossways*. The house and associated land stayed in the possession of the Deeres up to the death of Margery Deere in 1787, when it passed to Revd Henry Jones of Penmark (whose sisters were Elizabeth Jones of Llysworney and Mary Morgan, the wife of Revd John Morgan of Llanblethian).

Henry Jones died in 1795, leaving his estate to his wife Catherine for life. She let the house to a number of tenants, notably, from 1822 on, Robert Entwisle and his sister Margaret. Robert, brother of Hugh who moved into *Marlborough Grange* in 1838, was a retired colonel of the 61st Foot. He farmed *Crossways*, and not only as a mixed farm: a letter in 1831

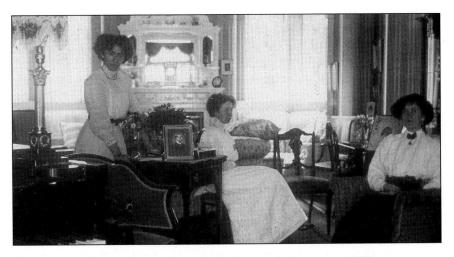

The Bassetts in the Drawing Room of Crossways, 1900

from Ann Thomas of *Hill House* to Mrs Jones, then living in Bath, stated: 'The garden at *Crossways* has been very productive of fruit. I have had a dozen and a half fine peaches from there; upward of a thousand taken off green from the trees'.

Catherine Jones died in 1837, and ownership of the property passed to Thomas Bassett of Bonvilston. In addition to Robert Entwisle, Thomas Lloyd also lived in *Crossways* in 1840. He owned a house near *Llanblethian Mill*, and was later referred to as being 'of Foxholes', the Entwisle family seat in Rochdale.

Robert died after a long and painful illness in 1847, and his sister continued as tenant, running the farm. The 1851 census described her as a farmer of 100 acres, employing three labourers and two boys. She retired from farming, and moved to *The Cross* about 1853; by 1859 Revd WH Beever farmed *Crossways*. Unusually for a headmaster of Cowbridge Grammar School, he was described as an expert on Shorthorns. He lived at the school, and had one of his workers – Robert Williams, aged forty-seven, born in Llantwit Major – residing in the house.

Twenty-eight-year-old Edward Thomas, Southerndown-born, farmed the 126 acres of *Crossways* in 1871, with the help of one man and three boys. Two live-in servants were also employed in the house for the family of husband and wife, two daughters and one son.

On the death of William Bassett in 1874, *Crossways* was left to his brother Richard of Bonvilston House, and Richard's younger son, Ralph Thurstan Bassett, was recorded as owner in 1877 and as occupier in 1881. He was born in Cheltenham in 1850; in 1881 he was described as a farmer, and in 1891 as a land agent. A wealthy man, he employed a governess for his two daughters, and seven servants. His daughters married well, Dorothy Sysyllt marrying the Hon Frederick Morgan, later to be fifth Baron Tredegar, while Olive married Roland Forestier Walker.

RT Bassett was a JP, Master of Foxhounds, and a prominent member of the gentry of the Vale of Glamorgan. He was responsible for the reconstruction of *Crossways* in the last years of the century, making it a very desirable residence.

Crossways was bought in 1906 (after the death of RT Bassett in 1903) by Anthony Miers of Bryntirion near Neath, and then sold on by him to William John Thomas, a colliery proprietor of Ynyshir in the Rhondda. The sale of the property by Sir WJ Thomas, JP, (for such had he become) in 1917 to Owen Williams, a shipowner, of Hendrescythan near Creigiau, marks the beginning of the most flamboyant period in the history of *Crossways*.

Owen Williams was from Edern in the Lleyn peninsula. He started life as a sailor on local coastal trading ships, but by 1899 he and his brother had founded the Silurian Steamship Company in Cardiff, and in the following year they set up the Golden Cross Line to run Mediterranean liner services and tramp services to Argentina. They prospered, and in 1917 the fifty-five-year-old Owen Williams married seventeen-year-old Margaret Thomas, the daughter of a Pontypridd mining engineer. It might seem that his wealth was a considerable attraction! Not only did he buy his father-in-law's exceedingly dirty mine, known locally as 'Dan's Muck Hole' (now buried under the Sardis Road rugby ground), but he also bought *Crossways House* and the associated land. Owen Williams expanded the *Crossways* estate by buying land from the Nash and the Rayer estates, and entered into farming with gusto, founding a celebrated herd of Hereford cattle, which won for him a leading position among British cattle breeders. He

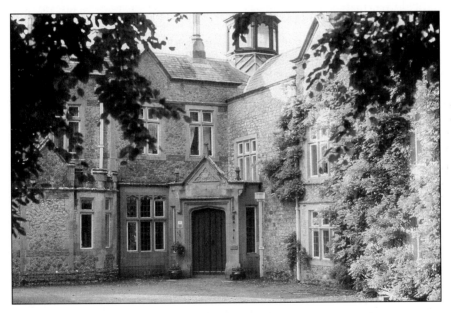

Crossways

was a good employer, with many jobs being created in the stables and stud, as well as the house and farms. Together with Thomas Thomas of *Stallcourt,* Owen Williams paid for a dinner concert for all returned servicemen of the district. This was held in *Cowbridge Town Hall* - 'a right old do it was. There was enough drink to have a bath in it' reported one of the participants.

Contemporary photographs of *Crossways* show that it was lavishly decorated and furnished, with eighteenth-century French furniture, Flemish tapestries, and Swansea and Nantgarw porcelain. Williams also extended the house, particularly the north wing, where the arch over what must have been a coachway still bears his initials, intertwined with those of his wife. No expense was spared on the house or on his young bride. On her twenty-first birthday, in 1921, Owen took Margaret to Cardiff docks to see one of his liners arrive from Italy. The deck was covered with a large tarpaulin and, when that was removed by a crane, a red Fiat sports car was uncovered - his birthday present to her.

By 1924 however, Owen found himself in very grave difficulties - agricultural, marital, and financial. His cattle were affected by disease, and could not be used for breeding, and so he could not recoup the inflated prices he had paid not only for pedigree horses and cattle but also for workaday animals. Prices slumped in the 1920s, partly because of general economic malaise and partly because the demand for horses fell in the face of mechanisation of transport and of agriculture. His wife ran away with an Indian nobleman, His Highness the Jam Sahib Sir Ranjit Sinjhi Vibhaji, the Jam Sahib of Nawangar, better known as the England cricketer Ranjitsinjhi. *Crossways* was mortgaged to him, and it must have been a bitter pill for Williams to swallow, to lose his wife and control of his house to a one-time friend. Finally, Owen Williams's wealth had been based on shipping, but freight rates had fallen drastically after the end of the war, and he had over-expanded his operations, and also bought unwisely.

The result of all this was the sale of the estate and farmland in 1924, and then of *Crossways* and its contents in December of that year. Owen Williams left the Vale of Glamorgan, laid up some vessels and sold others, and moved to London where he lived a solitary life, until he returned to Edern in 1930, with ten shillings in his pocket. It was a sad end to a varied and interesting life.

By 1930, *Crossways* had become the Prince of Wales hospital, a children's orthopaedic hospital. A newspaper report stated 'It was a pleasing revelation to the visitors to note the manner in which the stately old mansion had become adapted to such great and noble work. The patients – most of them tiny tots – looked radiantly happy'. The hospital also became a centre of nurse training, and some of the glass-fronted hospital ward remains incorporated into the present house.

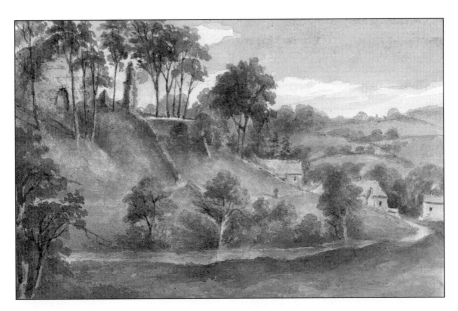

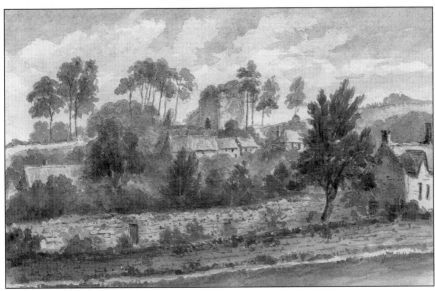

St Quentin's Castle and St Quentin's Hill
upper illustration from the north-west showing The Firs, the Mill,
and Brook House, lower illustration from the south
Watercolours by Col WH Taynton, 1852

INDEX

A selective index of families about whom some detailed information is available.